WHAT PEOPLE ARE SAYING ABOUT

THE NARROW WAY

The Narrow Way is the beautifully written and profound account of the difficult path Chris Lemig took to discover that we are all deserving of love and capable of true freedom. We can all find ourselves in, and benefit from, his journey.

Sharon Salzberg, author of *Lovingkindness* and *Real Happiness*

In *The Narrow Way*, Chris Lemig fearlessly slams his cinematic memoir down on your altar. He may go to India, but this ain't Eat, Pray, Love. *The Narrow Way* demands that you face the great secret: you cause your own suffering. But there's hope. Don't wait for the movie. Read this book!

Clayton Gibson, Founder of MyOutSpirit.com

In *The Narrow Way*, Chris Lemig reveals with poetic courage a life of struggle and suffering. There are no rounded corners here, just the author's bare, scarred innards. There is, however, a clear vision of a journey that must continue, and we are left rooting for Lemig as he adamantly wills together the broken pieces of his life.

Allan Lokos, author of *Pocket Peace: Effective Practices for Enlightened Living*

The Narrow Way is a journey into personal pain that is at once uncomfortable and deeply inspiring. Mr. Lemig shows us that it is the challenge of the human heart to find freedom, love and one's own way in the world.

Venerable Tenzin Kacho, a Tibetan Buddhist nun and co-author of *Rich Brother, Rich Sister*

The
Narrow
Way

A Memoir of Coming Out,
Getting Clean and
Finding Buddha

The Narrow Way

A Memoir of Coming Out,
Getting Clean and
Finding Buddha

Chris Lemig

**MANTRA
BOOKS**

Winchester, UK
Washington, USA

First published by Mantra Books, 2013
Mantra Books is an imprint of John Hunt Publishing Ltd., Laurel House, Station Approach,
Alresford, Hants, SO24 9JH, UK
office1@jhpbooks.net
www.johnhuntpublishing.com
www.mantra-books.net

For distributor details and how to order please visit the 'Ordering' section on our website.

Text copyright: Chris Lemig 2012

ISBN: 978 1 78099 749 0

A CIP catalogue record for this book is available from the British Library.

Design: Stuart Davies

Printed and bound by CPI Group (UK) Ltd, Croydon, CR0 4YY

We operate a distinctive and ethical publishing philosophy in all
areas of our business, from our global network of authors to
production and worldwide distribution.

CONTENTS

May this book be of benefit to others.
May it help those who are struggling with coming out.
May it ease some of the suffering caused by depression, alcoholism and addiction.
May it bring people hope that there are alternatives to suicide and that life can be filled with love, happiness and purpose.

Acknowledgments

Interdependence is one of the most beautiful and profound concepts in all of Buddhism. It tells us that nothing exists separately from anything else. Everything is connected.

When we look at a flower in a garden, our normal vision sees a lone object existing almost as if in a vacuum. But when we look a little closer, we see that the causes and conditions that bring that flower into being are inconceivably vast, like a jeweled web that extends into infinite space and time. Its myriad parts, the petals, the stem, the leaves as well as its color, shape and scent, all contribute to its unique expression. The flower is also dependent on the sun, the rain, the clean air, the worms, the soil and, not in the least, on the gardener who tends to it. It cannot exist without all these things working in concert.

Books are no different. Many gardeners have tended to this book and many people have, directly and indirectly, poured their hearts and souls into it and into me. To all of them, I am ever grateful.

First and foremost, I want to thank my mother and father for the gift of this precious human life. Without you I would not have had the opportunity to take this journey, to learn, to grow, and to ultimately change my life for the better. Thank you as well to my aunt, Sandy, for your limitless generosity, love, and support. You are one of my great inspirations. To Lynda, thank you for all of the love and encouragement you have shown me all these years. To Steve, Mandy and Ella, our adventure is only beginning. Thank you Caroline, Erik, JC, Bob, Nancy, Jen and Darcy, for always being there for me.

Many people helped with the sometimes painful process of creating and editing the final manuscript. Thank you to Dionne Howell and all the students of CNF 1 who gave me the confidence to begin this project. Thank you especially to Sue Van

Namee for your thorough and unflinching editorial comments. Without your insight this book would be even more confusing than it already is. Big thanks and love to Matthew Frum for checking my "Dharma-facts" and making sure that my rudimentary understanding of the Buddha's teachings would not be a source of confusion. Thank you, Brenna, for copyediting even as you faced all the demands of the end of your pregnancy. Best wishes to you and your new family!

Thank you to Mom, Dad, Lynda, Steve, Mandy, Zakary, Cindy, Galen, Sarah, Dave, Ben and Bruce and all of you who read the first of many "final" drafts, giving me much needed encouragement, advice and honest criticism.

Thank you to everyone at Ted's who supported me in my sobriety even while I continued (somewhat foolishly) to work with and around alcohol. I couldn't have done this without you.

To everyone at Thubten Shedrup Ling and Orgyen Khamdroling, my two Dharma homes, thank you for your inspiring spiritual practice.

Jess, may you always be happy.

Infinite thanks to my favorite gardener, my agent, Cicily Janus, for believing in this book from the beginning. Thank you for your kindness, your encouragement and your tireless efforts to bring it to publication.

To all my friends of the past, present and future, to all of those I have wounded, to all of you who have shown me so much kindness, love and patience, I thank you.

Last, to my precious spiritual teachers and guides, His Holiness the Dalai Lama, Anyen Rinpoche (and his tireless translator Allison Grabowski), Geshe Tsultrim Gyelsten, Geshe Sonam Rinchen, Chamtrul Rinpoche, Jetsunma Tenzin Palmo and Ven. Tenzin Kacho, may all of your spiritual aims be quickly and spontaneously fulfilled!

The Narrow Way

You are not alone. There are others, on the way on the same track. Travelers from nowhere to nowhere, on their way from nothing to nothing. The track may be narrow and steep and boring and frightening but everybody walks it. You are not alone but linked to everything around you. ~ Jan Willem Van De Wettering

Prologue

From this hour I ordain myself loos'd of limits and imaginary lines,
Going where I list, my own master total and absolute,
Listening to others, considering well what they say,
Pausing, searching, receiving, contemplating,
Gently, but with undeniable will, divesting myself of the
holds that would hold me. ~Walt Whitman

By all accounts I should be dead. But instead, through some miracle of chance or karma, I am alive. I do not pretend to even begin to understand how I came to wake up from my long and nightmarish sleep. Instead I just smile, a little dumbly and serenely, in the midst of the crowded airport as I wait for the long flight to India. In three hours I will head off on a pilgrimage, a spiritual quest that has been almost a year in the making. That leaves me plenty of time to think and wonder about this new arc that I am on, this upward spiral that for so long had sent me soaring down, down to a hard and hopeless bottom.

My old life comes into clear focus now. The free fall of eight thousand dark nights and blinding days. Countless hits and drinks and drags. The suicides, the self-sabotage, the shame. Twenty years of hiding, alone and afraid, and in the end all I had to show for it were the jagged shards of broken bonds and promises and dreams.

Was that really me? Was that my wake of destruction that I left behind? Would I ever be able to truly change and make amends?

Yes. It *was* me and I have already changed. As for amends, I will just have to wait and see.

I shiver and shake the memories off, safe on the firm earth for now. I look out the window onto the tarmac. The plane has already rolled up to the gate and the ground crew buzzes around like a stirred up hive of bees. They execute their synchronized dance of cleaning, restocking and refueling and my heart thumps louder and faster as I realize there is no turning back now. This is it. The moment of departure is at hand.

We are to fly up and over the top of the world, across Greenland then the Netherlands, arcing steadily over the brow of the earth until we roll down her eastern cheek like a tiny, shining tear. Fifteen hours from now New Delhi will come into view and I will press my nose into the glass like a ten year-old boy until it is mashed and sore. The lights of the city will fan out into the night and the humid air will be thick with the smoke of a million campfires. Still, the air will be good there, just as good as it is here and I will breathe it in, in great gasps fueled by the excitement and the shock and the fear of being in that strange place.

Then the air will turn thin and cool as I make my way up, up into the Himalayan foothills and the home of the Dalai Lama. It will feel good on my skin, chill and damp at night, and I will take it into my nostrils as I breathe slowly and surely in Dharamsala, learning again how to watch that simple thing, learning how to watch the breath.

I will wake in the early morning, in the cold and the dark, light candles and let myself be swept away by the spell of the melody of the deep mantras of the monks. I will walk in lock step with them for a pace or two on the path to liberation and I will see the goal clear and bright, so close that I will reach out and almost touch it.

Refreshed and renewed, I will make my way back down into the hot plains of great mother India and she will open her arms to me. There, I will follow in the footsteps of the Buddha. I will walk where he walked and see what he saw. There will be guides and signs and portents. There will be magic and mystery and illumination. Everyone and everything I come across will be my teacher. And though there will be hardship and I will cry for days, it will wring my heart free of all its toughness, until it becomes soft and pliant and I can finally put it to good use.

I catch my reflection in the glass and see that I am trembling now. Then I smile warmly at the new me and think: it's OK if none of this is true.

"We will now begin boarding flight two-nine-two with direct service to New Delhi," the attendant calls over the loudspeaker. The voice blows through my fantasies and daydreams and they collapse like a house of cards. It is real now. Whatever is to come is out of my hands. I feel the earth under my feet, solid and real. There is no time to waver, no time for remorse or even hope. It is time to take that first step. It is time to answer the call.

Chapter I

Apogee

Space flights are merely an escape, a fleeing away from oneself; because it is easier to go to Mars or the Moon than it is to penetrate one's own being. ~ Carl Jung

It is three years before India and I am not going anywhere. Instead, it is four in the morning and my eyes are wild and bloodshot as I pick through the carpet, searching for tiny pieces of crack cocaine that may have sizzled off the end of my pipe. My roommate sits on the bare floor of her room cooking up a fresh batch on a tarnished, blackened teaspoon but I can't wait to get another hit. I try to smoke what turns out to be the clipping of a dirty toenail, and it fills my mouth with the taste of burnt skin and rubber. Unfazed, I get up, light a cigarette and anxiously pace around the empty room. There is no furniture, no pictures on the walls; there are no mementos of vacations or framed photos of loved ones. Anything of any value has long ago been sold or traded for drugs. All that's left is a pile of bedding laid out on the floor next to an old lamp, its bare yellow bulb burning out like a dying star.

"This is gonna be a good one," Sarah says. I flop down cross-legged in front of her in childlike anticipation.

Out of a thin paste of cocaine, baking soda and water she has cooked off a dime-sized nugget of homemade crack. It's enough for three or four hits and she breaks me off a piece that I load into my pipe like there's no time to lose. I wave the flame back and forth until the rock starts to melt. I draw tiny puffs of air through the metal tube, careful not to suck the hot, molten goo through the wire mesh screen. The rock hisses and pops as it vaporizes and I pull in the hit as deep as I can.

"That's it. Hold it. Hold it. Just like that," Sarah says.

When I can't hold my breath any longer, I exhale a huge cloud of billowing white smoke that fills the space in front of me. It's at this moment that the high grabs hold of me, and it's like nothing I've ever felt before. My eyes roll back into my skull as my mind fills with the gong of an enormous bell. My body is flooded with the warm, golden tingle of a chemical orgasm that radiates through my belly, my head, my limbs. This is the soft oblivion I have been seeking, and now I am released from all my pain and doubt. My history is erased and it doesn't matter any more if I'm gay or not gay. Here, I don't have to face the truth of myself at all. I can drown the real me in the rush of the high, hold his head under the waters of it until he just quietly slips away. Here, all I have to do is wait for him to stop struggling and finally let go.

"Greg, Greg! GREG!!!" The scream from the living room below tears me out of my high. I peel myself off the floor, stumble out into the hall and down the dark stairway. I turn the corner to see my second wife slapping our lover hard across the face. He doesn't flinch. Instead, his body falls limply onto the moldy, beer stained couch. She props him up again and slaps him even harder.

On the coffee table, the sputtering light of a single candle dances on the face of an empty bottle of vodka. Long, thick lines of cocaine stand out white and sharp on a little slab of grey marble. A hundred pills of Xanax, Vicodin and Oxycontin, neatly twisted into a clear plastic baggie, look like Jolly Ranchers and gumdrops and I lick my lips at the sight of them.

"Is he breathing?" I ask.

"I don't know, I don't know, I don't know," she says biting her fingertips and sobbing.

I push her aside and lean in close to Greg's face. Through his nostrils I can hear a slow, thin wheezing. It's a relief. Even though we've been sleeping with him for months, I don't really care whether he lives or dies. All I really want to do is to keep getting high. I don't want to worry about ambulances or police or a lover overdosing on the couch in my living room. I stand over him for a few minutes until I can see the rise and fall of his chest. When I'm sure he's not going to die right then and there, I turn and walk away, back up the stairs and back to my pipe.

The months go by like one long day that will never end. Today I am drunk at a Thanksgiving dinner party when a friend gives me a tablet of methadone, the drug they give to heroin addicts who are trying to kick. But I am not trying to kick anything. I am trying to kill myself. The days of pacing myself are long gone so when ten minutes go by without any effect, I pound a bottle of wine then start in on the beer and shots. Soon I am a semi-conscious rag doll twisting, babbling and rolling around on the floor.

When I finally come to, I am standing in the middle of my own living room exhaling a huge hit of crack cocaine. I don't know how I got here. All I know is that every cell in my body is vibrating with pleasure. Then I seem to shatter open until I am weightless, without a body, mind or soul. There is no pain when there is nothing there to hurt.

The metal pipe is red hot and burns my fingers and lips and I pass it to my left before realizing there is a party going on. Then I come back to life, laughing, singing, dancing in circles and now and again collapsing on the floor. I take another hit, hold it deep in my lungs then kiss the guy next to me, blowing the smoke into his mouth.

When the drugs run out I turn to my stash of valium: six green pills that I take all at once, chewing them in my mouth and washing them down with warm beer. Soon I am cross-eyed, still wired from crack, but mellower and in a few hours I am again drunk and stoned enough to pass out into an uneasy sleep.

The afternoon sun intrudes through the sheets that I have duct taped around the windows. The drugs still stream through my veins, but it's no longer a pleasure buzz, just a jangling, grinding anxiety. Every muscle is taught and tense, ready to pounce. I force myself to stay in bed for another hour but all the things that I have to do, that I'm not doing, that I'll never do, roll through my head like an endless reel of a silent movie. Finally, I can't take it anymore and fling off the covers and head downstairs. I rummage through the overflowing ashtrays and find a half a cigarette, light it and inhale the stale smoke. I grab a beer out of the refrigerator and drink it in two gulps.

The buzz is coming on again when my wife comes home through the front door, and without a word she heads upstairs to our room to pass out. I hadn't really noticed she was gone but now that I do I am furious. After a half an hour of pacing around the house, guzzling beer after beer, I charge up the stairs. I find her already under the covers hiding her head from the bright Colorado sun, just trying to get a few minutes of sleep before she has to go to work.

"Where the fuck have you been?" I scream.

She throws back the covers wide eyes and naked. A sickening pleasure fills my belly like thick, sweet syrup that I swallow down with a great glug, glug, glug. I want her to be afraid. I want her to suffer. I want her to be ashamed. I need someone to blame. Someone who I can point the finger at for all *my* suffering, all *my* denial, all the injustice of *my* life. So I march around the room in a self-righteous fever, swinging my arms as I conduct a symphony of insults and abuse that I know will tear her down. Every intimate moment, every secret we ever shared, every confession of weakness, I dredge all of these out of my memory and throw them in her face. I tell her that she's no good, that she's worthless. I call her a liar and a cheater. I tell her that she can't take care of herself and that she wouldn't be anybody without me. With my eyes bulging out of their sockets and the spittle turning to foam at the edge of my mouth, the pitch climbs higher and higher towards its mad crescendo.

Finally, I call her a *whore* and tell her to get up and get out of *my* house. She looks at me like I've just stabbed her with a dull knife and twisted it in, smiling all the while. Somewhere deep inside I know that I should be falling on my knees and begging for forgiveness, but instead, my heart hardens completely and I just scream louder.

"Get out, get out, get out!"

She leaps out of bed, grabbing her purse and a handful of clothes. I follow her, still cursing and screaming. She trips down the stairs to the front door and when she turns to look back confused, hurt and broken, all I do is glare at her from the landing high above until she finally walks out.

Muttering, staggering, slurring I make my way to the kitchen downstairs. There is a bottle of vodka in the freezer and I begin to drink it straight in huge gulps that make me gag and spit up little mouthfuls of vomit. I walk back upstairs and knock on the door down the hall. Sarah is awake. She has heard everything. I pretend to cry on her shoulder for a while, pretend that I'm sorry for what I've done. Then I remind her that she owes me fifty dollars. She laughs and digs into her purse, pulling out a handful of crumpled bills and tosses them into my lap.

"You want me to call TJ?" she asks.

"Fuck it," I say. "Let's get some shit."

The drugs are delivered within the hour and I can't wait for the dealer to leave so I can lock myself in my room. It is late afternoon, but the sealed windows create the illusion of perpetual twilight. I load my pipe again and again while the soft moans from a porno ooze out of my television. The floor is covered with piles of dirty laundry, empty beer cans and cigarette butts. This is my life: a climax of disappointment thirty-five years in the making. I haven't even hoped for anything better for this in over a year.

I take a hit and inhale into oblivion, letting my eyes roll back until I forget who I am, who I was, who I might be. I hide, deny, evade and make another attempt at this futile escape. But there is no escape. Even though I have changed my name and moved once a year for the past eighteen years, even though I have changed my story and lied through my teeth, the truth has found me out every time. It tears through my body and mind like a chainsaw, unrelenting and agonizing.

I take another hit and feel a stabbing pain in my chest.

"This is it," I think. "This is the one that's gonna do it." And so I close my eyes, exhale and say a little prayer for the end.

Chapter 2

First Love

Hey Lover!

Is it ok if I call you that even though we never kissed? I hope so because that's what you were to me. I can finally see that now through the clear lens of time polished by the fine grit of too much anguish and suffering. We should have been together, should have shared so much more than we did, but the circumstances of time and place just wouldn't allow it. It's ok though. Time has closed the gap between us. At least in my mind.

Look at me, I'm rambling like a blushing schoolboy, just like I promised myself I wouldn't. But what am I supposed to say to you after all these years? How can I make you understand how important you were to me, even though nothing ever happened?

Do you remember that day as clearly as I do? Probably not. Maybe it wasn't the pivotal moment that I'm making it out to be. Maybe all this will only awaken in your mind a flash of light and memory, and maybe you'll smile and call me silly for making so much of it.

It was the beginning of fourth grade I think, and after four years we were still not used to the itch and scratch of starched, blue Catholic school shirts and ties. We clawed at the collars after kickball at recess and tore off the plaid nooses as soon as the last bell rang.

Billy came bursting into class that day and the commotion snapped all our heads up from the burning concentration of long division. He was panting and laughing and could barely contain himself. You came in after him with red cheeks too, grabbing his shirttail and trying to stop him in vain. I could see your fear, could see that you had been begging him not to tell all the way up from the damp basement lavatory, up the three flights of ancient steps, crying "please don't tell, don't tell, don't tell..."

But he was bigger than you, a sports jock even then, and faster, so he just laughed and sang as he taunted you up the stairs, "*I'm gonna tell, I'm gonna tell, I'm gonna tell...*"

And then I saw your shoulders slouch in defeat as you stood there on the stage as he rang out the proclamation that would call me home.

Two years before, in the high noon of East Coast summer when the air wrapped itself around me thick and hot, I had *my* theater debut. It was acting camp and it was the first time I had been pushed out of the nest on my own. My mother handed me off to a young woman of sixteen years and left me there bewildered and teary eyed.

"There, there," the young woman said and ushered me into the auditorium filled with the strange offspring of unfamiliar neighbors who wore funny clothes and smelled like Vienna sausages and wet dogs.

The workshop teachers, in bellbottoms and ponytails, divided us into groups that just made me feel more alone and afraid. I couldn't understand why the other children seemed so happy as they imitated the instructors, making animal noises and burping sounds and funny faces on cue. Every time my turn came, I just sat there silent, covering my face and wishing I would disappear.

But I didn't disappear and before I could protest one of the instructors stuffed a little white card into my hand and pushed me, along with all the others, into the long line that led up to the stage. On the card was a single word written in thick black letters and it felt heavy in my hands as I waited for my turn.

"You just get up there and act out the word for us," the young woman said. "And remember: Don't tell us...SHOW us!"

When she pushed me out from stage right into the glare of unwanted stardom, I froze. I looked down at my word, then back up at the hundred little faces that stared at me with wide, expecting eyes. But nothing came. I knew what I had to do but I couldn't do it. The image of the pose I should make burned in my mind's eye, but I was so choked with fear that all I could do was stand there hugging my sides, rocking my self back and forth while I looked down at my dirty sneakers and giggled.

"Shy!" a little girl shouted.

"Laughing!" another voice came.

One of the actors, a tall, deaf, bearded Jesus, came to pull me off the stage and out of sight. He was mute and so signed to me what to do. With a happy, encouraging grin he pushed me back out into the light. But still I stood there frozen, more afraid than before, terrified of being laughed at, of getting it wrong, as if even then I was afraid of being found out, as if even then there was some terrible secret that I was keeping from the world.

I felt the mass and heat of a body behind me. It was Jesus and he firmly grabbed my hands by the wrists and lifted my arms up until they were curved and flexing.

"STRONG!" came the cry in unison and they laughed while I cried as I melted back down into the crowd.

But I didn't feel strong at all, not that day and not the day when Billy burst into the classroom shouting:

"Jonathan just kissed me in the bathroom!"

A chorus of twenty ten-year old voices pealed with laughter, reveling in your shame as your arms dropped to your sides and your head hung down.

"Quiet, quiet!" shouted the nun, darting in and out of our desks like a one-woman riot police. But there was no controlling us. We all knew what Billy meant; we had whispered the word a hundred times in hushed giggles on the playground and pointed out who was and who wasn't. Now it was out and the class laughed and pointed their fingers at you and so did I. Better you than me, I thought.

I want to tell you how sorry I am about that. I'd like to say that if I could, I would travel back in time and trade places with you. I would do every thing I could to take away all that humiliation and embarrassment. I would take you into my arms and lead you out of there, away from the catcalls and the firestorm of shame. And then I would squeeze you hard and wipe away your tears and tell you over and over until you finally believed it:

"It will be ok, don't you worry. I promise. Everything will be ok."

Two years went by and finally we graduated from old Saint Mary's. Then it was off to public school, junior high and the real world for us. We stayed in touch for that first year, but gone were the sleepovers that you and Billy would come to on hot summer nights. Do you remember those? We camped out in the attic of Dad's garage, daring one another to show it. But no one ever did. I remember how you smelled, the sweat of your armpits both revolting and enticing. I remember too, watching you breathe in the moonlight after you fell asleep, wanting so bad to pet your soft cheek without knowing why.

But then the day came when I realized what that feeling welling up in my belly had been all about. It tore and clawed at me to get out as I rubbed and rubbed against anything and everything within my reach: shag rugs and blankets, plush animal toys and trees. I tried to hump the world, humped it raw all to the tune of the visions of all the girls I'd come to know, imagining them in all their soft and bumpy glory. But nothing ever happened, and all I ever got was chaffed and sore.

Still I kept at it, diligent to the end until one day the memory came flooding back. There you were in the dark damp basement of St. Mary's with Billy standing at the urinal, whistling with his fly unzipped. Then, as if possessed by some mischievous spirit and in some fit of uncontrollable glee, you leaned in and kissed him, wet and warm on the cheek.

I saw him in my mind as he pulled back in shock, and as he did I came full of force and pleasure and golden light. The revelation that boys could love boys came in the form of a tidal wave that flooded over my bed sheets, and I didn't know whether to jump up for joy or run away in terror. When it was over I cleaned up that glistening and mysterious pool of me, head still spinning from the mad delight of it all, knowing that once and for all I was a different creature.

I don't mean to embarrass you but I thought about you every day after that. As the months went by my crush became an aching and it threatened to squash me like a bug. I had to do something. So one summer day I picked up the phone, palms sweating and body shaking. When you answered I could hardly move my lips and the air leaked out in a thin, squeaking "Wanna come over?"

"Sure!" you said and my heartbeat went rat-tat-tat like a snare drum tapping out the staccato rhythm of lust.

It took you almost two hours to ride your bike all the way from New London, and I spent the whole time staring out the window, waiting for you to roll around that corner. By the time you arrived I must have looked a terrible mess: pale, sweating and trembling with fever. You let your bike fall into the fresh cut grass and walked towards me through the thick air of summer that was filled with the love song of birds and wind and ocean.

"Wanna look at some dirty magazines," I blurted.

"Sure," you said again and I thought "This is it; it's really going to happen."

So up to my room we climbed with me holding your hand, and I pulled out the stash of Hustlers and Penthouse that I had long ago pilfered from my Dad's closet. We lay out on my bed and flipped through the glossy pages together. You sneered a little in disbelief that people's bodies could really do things like that. Your naiveté filled me with a surge of confidence, and I was sure that you would do anything I asked.

"Do you know how to masturbate?" I finally said in an overture of love. It was a great leap into the unknown, and I waited, afraid to move or even breathe, as the birds and the grass and the ocean and the wind all leaned up close to my window and waited too.

"No!" you said with your face twisted into a contortionist act of disgust. "That's a sin!"

Did my face twist then too? Did you see my watering eyes filling slowly with disappointment and disgrace? We were on stage again, but this time it was me that everyone was laughing at, pointing their fingers and crying, *pansy, pansy, he's a little pansy* in that singsong revel that every generation learns anew.

My heart broke right then and there. You weren't gay at all. You didn't want to have anything to do with me. And so it was you that stood by me that day as I took my first step into the closet and it would be years before I saw you again.

Chapter 3

Homecoming

It is mid afternoon in Dharamsala. The hills are shrouded in mist. It is dreamtime and mystery weather in one of the wettest places in India.

I have come here to find clarity, to follow the calling in my heart, to see His Holiness the Dalai Lama, to spend time in retreat, and to use this place as a stepping off point for my pilgrimage of ten thousand miles. But only two days off the plane from the West, and I am already disoriented and bewildered by the barrage on my senses. Everywhere I turn there is noise, poverty, pollution, disease. Families cram into three walled shacks on the sides of the road. Women make fuel for their fires out of patties of dried dung and straw. Oxen carts loaded high with bales of hay and cloth lumber down the freeways while the trucks and cars barrel by. Lepers with missing fingers, toes and limbs reach out for alms. The gritty air tastes like diesel and smoke while the heat of it burns my lungs.

All of these sights, sounds and smells assault my tiny, sheltered world view, a world view shaped by years of stubbornly shutting all of these things out, of stomping my feet and beating my chest: *No one suffers like me! I am the most miserable of them all!* But now the reality of the world sweeps that little me away and I have to wonder: who is left?

So I am fresh and new as I take my first steps out of Green Hotel and onto Bagshu Road. I curl my soft, pink toes in close as the wheels and feet and hooves crash by. I could lie down end to end twice and be at the other side but still, on this narrow holy highway, half the world has gathered. It is lined with the market-place of heaven and earth: a cornucopia of silk and fruit, malas and beads, Buddhas, vajras and bells. Monks and nuns with cell phones and laptops hurry from end to end, speeding up the illumination of the world. The air is filled with a great communication of howling, honking and haggling. The poor, the wealthy, the newly born and the dying all push and tug and grab at my sleeves, and I pull away as I push deeper into the throng. A thousand faces blur across the field of my vision, and in this waking dream they are Indian, Tibetan, German, Israeli, Chinese, American, English and Dutch and I smile at each one with a goofy, toothy grin.

"Well here I am!" I want to say. "I have arrived and now we can meet again for the first time. Now we can become fast friends just like we were meant to be!"

I think we are supposed to rejoice now and sing together because we have all come here, finally, to take our first steps on the spiritual path, to once and for all wake up from this terrible dream. Why else would we be here? But no one seems to remember this but me and so instead, they all look through me like I am some apparition of a stranger, just another foreigner who doesn't belong.

But I am not afraid. I am hard and fierce in my resolve and I keep going, out of the center of town, leaving the crowded streets behind until the road turns into nothing more than a footpath. It takes me through the Himalayan forest, through groves of arthritic pines knotted, twisted and bent from the winds of a hundred monsoons. I make my way up until I come to a high archway topped with two golden deer facing a brilliant wheel that shines like the sun and I pass under them.

The Tibetan Institute of Performing Arts. This is the first stop on my long list of things to do, places to see, adventures to have. It seems an easy first step, a primer for things to come. I have been here many times already, watched myself in my dreams come up this forested hillside, find my way to the theater and sit down next to forgotten kin from a dying land. I have sat wrapped in joy and wonder as the lamas danced out the long dream-stories from the past that they will never forget. I have wept at the operas of love and loss that all soar ultimately to climaxes of spiritual triumph. I have been mesmerized by the costumes of turquoise and pluming red and gold. I have watched the human story unfold in a language I have never heard, yet somehow, have understood it all.

But today it is quiet and grey. The open courtyard is almost empty except for a handful of young Tibetans in ripped jeans and Kurt Cobain t-shirts. They practice their instruments, bulbous lutes with fat, sinewy strings that wobble and warble and drone. They sing a few bars of traditional songs and the melodies drift up over the tops of the trees where the wind catches them and carries them north over the mountains and back home.

They do not notice me as I scuttle from building to building, jiggling locked door handles until finally, one of them opens. Inside a draughty, dark room a young Tibetan woman sits behind an old, warped desk stacked high with envelopes and papers. She does not look up.

"Are there any performances scheduled this month?" I ask.

"Nothing for the rest of the year," she says to the desk. The bright dream of dancing lamas pops like a soapy bubble in my face and the spray and the shock of it wakes me up.

Where am I? How did I get here? I rub the sleep out of my eyes, back my way out of the office on tiptoe, back into the courtyard. It is still and deserted now. The students are gone if they were ever there at all. There is no dream music, no performance, no story unfolding. All is silent and I am alone.

Little waves of panic wash over me. What am I doing here? Who do I think I am? I am no hero on pilgrimage, no Basho, no bodhisattva on holiday; I am just a tourist, naked and naïve in a place far away from home. My knees turn to jelly and as I run for the archway it only seems to get further and further away.

The mist has turned thick and heavy, and now it sheds fat drops of cold rain that soak my hair and stream down my face. I hurry down the hill hoping that I will make it back to my room before my tears outnumber the raindrops.

I trip in a pothole and grab at the air to catch my balance. Up and to my left a group of homeless lepers, unconcerned by the rain, watches the curious westerner, lopping down the path, looking sad and lost. One of them leans on a makeshift crutch. He only has one leg. Before I can turn away our eyes meet. I wonder if he can see into the very heart of me, if he sees all my anxiety and worry. I want him to judge me, to slap me hard across the face and shock me out of this bout of self-pity. But instead, he holds my gaze and offers me a wide smile. Then he brings his hands together in the gesture of blessing and prayer.

"Namaste! Be happy, sir!" he shouts over the *thwapping* din of raindrops while the light in his eyes flashes like lightening.

I am struck dumb and all I can do is give him an insincere smile of my own. I am not ready to believe that life can be this good and simple, and so I flee back to my hotel to retreat and to hide.

I burst through the door, throw myself on the hard mattress. The walls of my tiny damp room that reek from fifty years of monsoon mildew close in around me. The noise from the street outside my window turns into a deafening symphony of cows and dogs and rickshaws all honking and snarling and mooing in seven different languages.

"I am here! I am here! I am here!" they all say.

I wrap a pillow around my head to block out the noise and close my eyes tight, but the reality of India cannot be held at bay with a stuffed sack of cotton batting. The cacophony is an all-pervasive hum now, and as I force myself to drift off into an uneasy sleep, all I can see in my mind's eye is the one-legged man smiling at me in the rain.

When I wake just after dawn, I am still in India. I have not been miraculously transported home. I do not rub my eyes and see all the familiar shapes of my old room coming into focus. Instead, I see the yellow walls, damp and crumbling. I feel the hard cotton mattress cutting off the circulation in my hips and the cold stone floor under my bare feet. It is the dream that is real and I have no choice but to face this day.

I look for my resolve that was swept away by the torrent of yesterday's culture shock, find it only a little way downstream on a sandy bank. I pick it up, brush it off, see that it is still shiny and good. I put it in my pocket for safekeeping and remind myself not to let it go so easily next time.

I pull out a slim, brown notebook from my pack. Across the top, in fat, black marker pen, I have written a title. *The Golden Thread.* It is my handmade book of hours, a collection of quotes from a year of study back home. They are messages in bottles and breadcrumbs to lead me out of the maze of my own fears. The Buddha has sprinkled little gems here and there, some of them no more than a few words. There is pith advice on meditation and staying in the present moment. There are gentle reminders to think of others, especially if all I'm thinking about is myself. Lines of wisdom from His Holiness the Dalai Lama and other great masters of India, Japan and Tibet are woven in with the poems, prayers and ringing insights of Henry David Thoreau, Joseph Campbell, Walt Whitman and Saint Francis of Assisi. These are my new heroes and as I read a few verses they reach out to me from the thin pages to lift me back to my feet.

"Do not quit!" say all the Buddhas and those who have come before me. So I put on earphones and music and sing to myself. Then I dig out a real needle and thread, sew on an old button that dangles off my pants. The mundane victory is enough and once again I am standing on solid ground.

The sun is shining today and the retreating monsoon is nowhere to be found. Gone are yesterday's mists and rain, and I prop open the door to my room, taking in a deep breath of the cool morning air. Rich smells from the Green Hotel's kitchen waft up to my balcony and my stomach rumbles. I haven't eaten in over a day. So I sling on my shoulder bag and skip downstairs to fill my belly with *tsampa*, a kind of Tibetan barley porridge, honey and milk tea.

Now I dive back into the bustle of McLeod Ganj refreshed and fortified. Lepers still line the sides of Bagshu Road but now I don't look away. Instead, I drop a few rupees into each of their hands, some of which have been gnawed away by their disease into smooth stumps, and we exchange warm smiles. They are not the other anymore. They are just people. Potential friends.

At the bus stand I take a hard right onto Tushita Road, a winding alley ravaged by years of torrential rains that leads up into the hills. The way narrows and steepens and soon I am sweating and short of breath.

After twenty minutes, I reach the outer gate of Tushita, the Buddhist retreat center that I will soon be living at for ten days. The hill, densely wooded with pine trees, is swarming with monkeys. They leap from tree to tree and sometimes break out into violent skirmishes. A young monk in red robes hovers tentatively at the gate, pacing back and forth. I wave to him but he doesn't wave back.

"Are you going to Tushita?" he asks.

"Yes," I say.

"Good, good. We should walk up together then. The monkeys will be less likely to attack two of us." He stoops down and picks up a handful of small stones and hides them under his robes.

As we walk slowly up the steep, winding steps, I try to block out visions of bloody carcasses being ripped to shreds by packs of rabid primates. We keep our eyes down, trying not to make eye contact, especially with the large alpha males who watch us too closely. When one of them makes a sudden rush towards us, crashing through the limbs of the trees above, the monk pulls out a stone and throws it into the forest. It ricochets loudly through the branches and the aggressor backs off. For the rest of the way we are left alone, and we soon leave the tribe behind to forage and preen in the growing warmth of late morning.

We reach the top of the stairs and I am suddenly in a different world. The air is crisp in these high foothills, fresh from the previous day's rain and scrubbed clean by pine needles. A circle has been cleared on the top of the hill that overlooks the wide, rolling plains to the south. Sturdy dormitories and administration buildings with fresh coats of red and white paint form a crescent around the clearing. In the middle of the complex is a giant gompa, a meditation hall two stories high, surrounded by gardens and flowerbeds and green lawns. Gone are the trash, sewage and debris of the town below. Gone too is the noise and the silence shocks me into the present moment.

Stillness, serenity, solitude. These are what I have come here for and I breathe it all in and close my eyes.

Besides my monk friend, only a few figures move quickly and quietly from one building to the next. But then, with a short wave goodbye even he leaves me, hurrying around a corner and out of sight on his unknown errand.

But I don't mind being alone, not here. In this place, I feel immediately welcome and at ease. I fold my arms around my back and begin a slow, reverent walk around the gompa. With each step I begin to feel light and free. I have made it. It is a small miracle, but after traveling halfway around the world, I have found my way with nothing but a vague map and a guidebook to this tranquil hillside retreat.

Around the south side of the gompa, the grounds open up into a terraced yard with wide stone steps and flowerbeds. A Tibetan pole flag flaps in the wind, its edges frayed from years of sending out prayers of love and compassion to all beings. Down below and to the left is an ornate stupa sitting serenely and majestically on the green lawn. It is a monument to the Tibetan teacher who founded this place over thirty years ago. I am overcome with emotion at the sight of it and I stumble over to the gompa steps to collapse. I am stunned awake and I can't believe my eyes. *I have been in this place before.*

Suddenly, everything makes complete and perfect sense. All the jagged pieces of the puzzle that is my life now slide together with ease. I have been led here, drawn here by some magnetism of the spirit, by some force that I can't see or touch or feel, but that I know resides right here before me. I am certain, beyond all doubt, that every step since my birth has been on the path to this very place. All the years of addiction and suffering in the closet were necessary side journeys and pit stops along the way. But now, I am exactly where I need to be.

"I am home," I say. "I am home after being lost for so long."

Time slows, then stops altogether and I sit here with the warm sun on my face for a little moment of eternity. All the effort that I've put into getting here has been worth it and it feels like I've set down a heavy load. I let out a long, quaking sigh before taking one last look around.

I find my way back to the path and start the long hike down the hill. The monkeys are gone now and the forest is quiet. I pull out my mala, a string of beads for counting prayers, and start saying the only mantra I know. *Om Mani Padme Hum.* It seems like such a familiar thing to do, like it's something I've done a million times before. But I haven't. Not in this life anyway. So I recite that mantra over and over as I walk back into town until the melody resonates deep in my mind. I say it out loud even as I pass travelers coming up the other way. I chant it softly to myself as I come back around the corner into the middle of the lunacy of the bus stand. I say it while smiling at the lepers and the monks and the tourists I pass along the road. I say it all the way back to the Green Hotel. I say it as I climb up the stairs to my damp little room. I say it a hundred times, a thousand times, like I'm making up for too much lost time. I say it like there's no time to lose.

Chapter 4

Diagnosis

"Christopher-Michael-Lemig-Jr.!"

The serrated voice tears through the air, up the stairs, into the private world I am building there and I know that I am in trouble again.

I put on my mask of rock 'n roll and screaming for vengeance that hides all my fear and trembling. These days, at fourteen years old with a pack of Lucky Strikes hidden close to my skin, I sneak hard liquor from the dining room cabinet. With shaking fingers I pull the bottles from the back, oh so careful not to clink them together in the still night. Then I smuggle them out in the folds of denim and leather, one by one into the woods behind the house, where the little sips of scotch and gin burn just enough to soothe the pain that gets worse every day.

Have I been forgotten as the storm of confusion and hormones and growing up different rages on in me and around me? The only calm is out there in those tangled woods of barbed briars and sumac where I hide from divorce, from remarriage, from the homophobic racist stepfather who has moved in calling himself Lord. Out there, by the cool spring that bubbles up pure and clean, I listen for some faint whisper: that it's ok to be me, that it's ok to like boys more than girls.

But the spring never speaks. It just bubbles and babbles and I think: *oh well, at least it never runs dry.*

I tumble down the stairs now, and when I turn the corner my mother is standing in the kitchen five feet tall and terrible. My mother, once the source of all my comfort, now the source of all my fear.

"What are these for?" she asks.

There, in her open palm, rest the two wrapped condoms I had

hidden safe and secret like precious coins: the fare for the ferry boat that would one day take me across the wide river to the shore of the real thing. I had quaked and shivered all over when my best friend, Mike, dropped them onto the bed between us and I gasped in wonder.

"These are for sex!" I thought. And as I picked them up, the revelation was a heavy, holy grail right there in my two little hands.

But now I am silent and the glossy plastic rings shine before me even as I try with all my will to tear my gaze away.

"Is Mike gay?" comes the wrong question that we both know the answer to. Her eyes smolder and I shudder and I know that it is the worst thing a boy can be.

"No, no, no!" I cry. While the *yes, yes, yes!* echoes inside then fades away, even as the budding new part of me that I've been grappling with, alone in the dark, cries to get out. All my daydreams of dressing up in stockings and high heels and rolling around in laughing little games with my boyhood crushes flash in front of me. But I am so afraid and I think: *oh my god, she can never know, she will never understand.* So I tell myself that these daydreams belong to another boy, some strange boy from far away, and the moment slips by.

And so with a shake of her head she sends me back to my room with her sobs following behind me as I trudge back up the stairs and quietly shut the door.

A day goes by, then another and another. They are all dark days filled with a shame that seasons the steely blood that flows in my mouth from biting my tongue. The question has been asked, however obliquely, and I know now that no one really wants to know the answer.

There is no need to say it anyway. You see, my family doesn't communicate in words but instead, by directly transferring thoughts from mind to mind. My stepfather has this power too, so when I see him and my mom eyeing me darkly across the dinner table, I can hear what they are thinking.

"What is wrong with him?" they say.

"I'm gay," I tell them. But they never listen.

Then comes the day I come home from school and my mom is crying in the living room. Her new husband, the Lord, is there comforting her with her head buried in her hands while the tears drip, drip, drip through the cracks of her fingers.

"There, there dear, everything will be ok," he coos.

Then he turns and looks me up and down with hatred and disgust that makes me wish I could disappear into the walls and the wood and never come back out.

"I'll deal with you later you filthy little pervert," he tells me with his mind.

I run up the stairs to lock myself in my room, my sanctuary, but when I get to the top and push open the door the blood drains out of me and into the floor. My bed is overturned. All my dresser drawers have been tossed around and emptied. My locked file cabinet, my treasure chest of adolescent mysteries, has been pried open and all the secret, sacred contents looted. Everything has been found: the cigarettes, the liquor, the pornography, the dildos, the stockings.

It's not me, it's not me, it's not me, it's not me. But when I open my eyes again the mantra hasn't worked and nothing has changed.

But then the panic subsides. I take a deep breath. I relax and let go. Now they know. They must know. Now I am transparent and all of my longing is known to the world. There is nothing left to hide.

They are standing behind me now and they take me by the arms, march me down the stairs, out into the light of day where the neighbors wonder and whisper behind closed doors and tightly pulled curtains. For a moment, when the sun hits my face, I think that they are going to set me free, to let me flap my wings and finally fly high and away into the clear sky. But instead I am only being led to another cage.

In the silence of the back seat of the old blue Pinto, the shadows of oak and maple flutter across my face. We twist and turn through the winding country roads until we leave the comfort and shelter of home and enter the big city of New London. There is concrete here and crime and drugs and poverty. There are psychiatrists, too.

My psychiatrist waits for me behind a windowless door in a pre-fab office building that smells of fresh paint and carpet glue. His name is painted on the door in gold letters: Dr. Gary Greenburg, PhD. But in 1984 on the eastern shore of the United States it may as well read "witch doctor".

I am naked and exposed in the florescent light of the hallway as my mother knocks on the door. I am humiliated and powerless even as rage boils in my belly. I cannot breathe. The pressure has nowhere to go. I am going to implode.

The door opens with a swooshing and sucking of air from the hallway. It draws the air out of me too, and I breathe again with a sudden gasp. Dr. Greenburg is smiling on the other side as he holds the door open and waves us both in. He is skinny, frail, with pale thin arms and a narrow face. His wispy black hair falls into his eyes so he has to brush it away when he turns his head. His eyes are nut brown and warm. He is no witch doctor that I have ever imagined and when I look at him I feel safe.

"Thank you Mrs. Lord," he says. "I've got it from here."

We leave her, befuddled and dumfounded, in the waiting room and he points me to a comfortable chair. He pulls up a seat right in front of me and kicks off his shoes. Then he crosses his legs and looks at me with those dark brown eyes, wide and friendly and full of care.

"So, what's going on?" he asks.

With a great exhale I let down my defenses, open the gates and let him in. I divulge. I confess. But it is confession without guilt, without penance or remorse. There are no sins here, only the beginnings of trust and truth. I don't know where the words come from, didn't know I had so many words dammed up inside me, but they flow out now like a river and all the confusion of my young mind takes shape right before my eyes. Dr. Greenburg does nothing. He just listens, holding up a mirror so I can see it all, so I can see who I am without the judgment and the fear and the self loathing that have already become reflexes, taut and fine tuned.

When the session is over, I am smiling. There is nothing wrong with me after all. Dr. Greenburg slaps me on the shoulder and I laugh for the first time in a year. But when he opens the door and I see my mother waiting outside with deep lines of worry on her face as she waits for the diagnosis, my heart sinks into darkness again.

It is appointment day and I am looking forward to my third session. The resentment and the stigma of going to the doctor are gone. In only two weeks he has become my psychiatrist and I even brag to my friends about where I go every Wednesday after school. Maybe today he will ask me about being gay, I think. Maybe today I will tell him the whole truth. That is what I really want, someone to just come out and ask the question, point blank, like a gunshot or a sucker punch. I would welcome it.

"Well, are you gay?" they will ask. "Yes," I will say and be embraced again, and loved. No more innuendos and awkward avoidances. No more shushing up the obvious; no more uneasy evasions. No more mind reading. No more silence.

I come down from my room and find my mom poring over bills and letters at the kitchen table.

"Well, are we going?" I ask pretending that I don't really want to.

"No," she says.

I wait for more, some reason or explanation, but there is just the wide gap of silence between us. I can hear the scratch of pen on paper, the cat clawing at the screen door behind me, the mail truck idling outside the open window. The warm air of late spring carries in the scent of honeysuckle and sea that used to fill me with joy, calling me and my little brother out to play boyhood games, simple in their rules and enjoyment. But now I just feel nauseated and recoil as I look over the edge of this new cliff.

"Why?" I whisper.

She slams down her pen, huffs and puffs before blowing my house down.

"Oh c'mon!" she says. "We can see you have *Dr. Greenburg* bamboozled just like the rest of us!"

I see. I am a liar now.

And that is that. I have tried to tell the truth; was forced to tell the truth. But it was not the truth that anyone wanted to hear. The message is now seared in my mind: To tell the truth is to lie; to lie is to tell the truth. So I give up on the truth and I seal myself away. My little secret self that everyone now knows but denies is even there will be routed back to the forest and the dark. I will be silent again. I will speak to no one. I will forget the passwords that let even friends through the gate and I will be alone.

Chapter 5

Silence

On a quiet night, mutely sitting in a temple,
Infinite silent solitude reveals myself in itself.
Losing futile thoughts,
Alas, here is the Buddha! ~ Zen Poem

Now I have come to the shore of great silence. The young boy who ran to hide in the woods all those years ago has traveled so far to come here. How much noise there was along the way! I remember screaming out loud to the deaf sea and sky, trying to drown it all out. I remember too, muffling the din with the heavy, wet blanket of drunk and stoned. Finally, desperate and hopeless, I even offered myself to be swallowed up by what I thought would be the final silence of death. But in the end I pulled back from those gapping jaws and now, in the relative quiet of sobriety, I have come here to finally listen to the sound of my true self. No more endless chatter, I say! No more telling myself lies and stories and half-truths. No more chasing the tails of thoughts that loop round and round, thoughts that go on and on without end or purpose.

Here in Tushita, I see there are other travelers who have followed the call of silence. They come up the steps loaded down with heavy packs in ones and twos, and soon there are nearly fifty of us gathered at the entrance to the retreat center. We catch our breath as we dab the sweat from faces and foreheads after the long climb. The clear, high voice of this place has gone far and wide across the earth and now we all gather at the top of the hill under the shade of cool pines, wide eyed and wondering. Why have we come here? What do we hope to find? The air crackles and sizzles with the electricity of our expectations.

As I look around at all these new faces, I realize that I am not alone after all and this makes me smile. It is good to know that there are so many others who want to spend time in retreat, to spend ten whole days of their hard earned leisure time at this course on meditation and Buddhism. I think too that I am glad that we are in a high place. All retreats should be in high places, or maybe by the sea. Either way we need to be close to the source of ourselves, far and away from the noise and confusion that always pulls us in a million directions at once.

"We're going to begin the registration now," a young Swiss woman calls out over the tops of our heads. We have been dancing gingerly around each other to the tune of polite introductions but now it is time to get serious and we all snap to attention. "Please be patient as you are a bigger group than usual. We will call your names in the order that you signed up for the course."

I tense and stiffen, wait and worry. Is my name really on that list? Did I fill out the registration form right? Has there been some terrible mistake? I may be clear-headed and sober now, but the old me, the me that doesn't believe in himself, is still there, still fighting to run the show.

"Christopher...LEEMEEG?" I laugh out loud. Of course I was the first to sign up, months before any of the others. I marked my calendar long ago, ticked off the days when sign-up would begin, set my alarm clock to India time so I would wake at that exact moment. I had left nothing to chance.

So now I head to the dining hall. It has been set up like an assembly line and we stop at one table after another. We sign waivers and pay fees. We drop cameras and cell phones and MP3 players into big plastic bags that are whisked away to be locked in the center's safe, shedding the noisemakers like unwanted, dead skin. Then there are rules and regulations to agree to, rooms to be assigned, maps to look over.

"Does that watch have an alarm?" the young man behind the

last table asks.

I squint at his nametag. John, it says. I hold up the fancy watch like a game show host.

"John, this thing will scramble eggs if I ask it to..."

He doesn't laugh; he just blinks at me through his wire frame glasses then looks back down at the list in front of him. "Karma Yoga Jobs" it reads across the top and then I feel a little ashamed at my silly joke, like already I have broken the silence.

"Good, you can be the morning gong ringer then. Meet me outside the front of the gompa in an hour and I'll show you what to do."

The Gong Ringer! It sounds so important, so official! The shame I felt only a moment ago is swept away by the pride that swells over its banks, and I polish my knuckles on my chest as I follow the little map up the hill to my room. Only a year ago I was smoking cigarettes and drinking myself half to death, but now I am here in India and I am already The Gong Ringer!

My dorm room is on the very edge of the grounds. I slip the old skeleton key into the keyhole and pry the door open with a resounding creak that echoes up the hillside. The plain, unpainted room is crowded with four squat bed frames that my roommates and I will toss and turn on for the next ten days. Above one of them, on a corner shelf that hangs on the wall, is a tiny stone Buddha. He beckons me serenely from the other end of the room and as I sit down on the edge of the bed I laugh. It is a typical India mattress, a thin cotton futon that long ago had all the comfort squashed out of it. I smack it with a satisfying *thwap* and lay down. If it is good enough for the Buddha to watch over, it is good enough for me.

My first roommate arrives. He is from the States too, lives only a few miles from me in fact, and it takes a minute for the coincidence to sink in before we burst out laughing at the strangeness and the wonder of it all. Then the silence returns uninvited but welcome and we sit for a long while, both smiling out the door at the trees and the monkeys that squabble and scream out there.

At one o'clock my watch beeps softly. Time to learn how to ring the gong.

John is waiting for me outside the huge black doors of the gompa. He plants his feet firmly on the ground as he grabs a big iron ring and pulls hard. I follow him in, eyes glued to him, not wanting to miss a thing. He shows me where the bronze bell and cotton mallet hang just inside the great hall filled with the yellow light of the sun. Then he takes me outside again and shows me how to hit it just right so the warm, round tone resonates softly through the quiet of the retreat grounds. He shows me the other spots to do this. Three times a day for the next week and a half: for waking up, breakfast and the morning's teachings. He tells me that this will be a way for me to not only be mindful but also to be of service to everyone else here on retreat. I look around and see all the other seekers learning their tasks. Some will sweep the floors, clean the toilets, wash the dishes, help with meals. I take the bell from him humbly now and try for myself until I get it right.

We all meet again inside the meditation hall. A great circle of well-worn cushions, *zafus* and *zabatons*, radiates out from the center. Kunpen, the young German nun who runs this place, is poised on one of them. For some reason she doesn't look strange at all, this western woman in red robes and a head shaved smooth and white like an egg. She smiles and waits for the gaggle to settle onto the strange bulbous seats and we wiggle and wobble until we find our balance.

She begins with the certainty and confidence of a merchant ship's captain as she starts to tally off the long list of rules and expectations. We have already read most of them but now, as the nun reads them off of a bulleted list, they sound more daunting than ever before. This is the real thing and there is no turning back.

We are to wake at six every morning and be ready for our first meditation session at six forty-five. Then a short breakfast of fruit, porridge and tea. Buddhist teachings begin at nine and will last late into the morning. There will be yoga and the stretching of tired limbs each day just before lunch. Free time after this should be filled with study and meditation, we are told. More teachings will follow until dinnertime. Then we will meditate until nine or nine thirty at night.

While we are here there will be no talking, no smoking, no drinking, no sex. There will be no lying, no stealing, no killing, not even of insects. We are to live as though we are monks and nuns in training and the thought of this gives me a little thrill. But as I look around at the other faces in the room I see watering eyes and gaping jaws.

Kunpen sees these too and she lets out a peal of laughter that sets us all at ease.

"Don't look so glum," she says. "It's not as bad as all that!"

Then she tells us jokes and stories from past retreats and her eyes tell us to have light hearts, to have faith in ourselves, that we can do this.

"The silence will begin after dinner tonight," she reminds us at the end. "Please take the vow of silence seriously; you will find that it is more difficult than you imagined."

But the warning fades away as we file into the dining hall. Soon it is buzzing with conversation. Everything is all so new and exciting. Even the simple vegetarian meal of soup, bread and butter seems a great feast. The dining hall bustles with all of this as we take advantage of one last chance to speak to one another. But then one by one, we get up from the long tables and take our plates to the dishwashers. Our voices fade to a few scattered whispers then to no sound at all.

We meet back in the gompa, the new center of our lives, and find that the cushions have been set up in neat rows facing the great altar occupied by the images of a hundred different Buddhas. A man sits on a cushion just under all of these. He faces us, his cushion slightly higher than the rest. He is not dressed in robes, his head is not shaved, nor does he have a thousand arms or a halo around his head. He looks like he could be any one of us. But then I look more closely at his face. He is smiling and serene like no one I have ever seen before. There is no pretension anywhere to be found. Neither is the smile a mask hiding a half secret fear or contempt. He is completely present and in him I sense no wish to be anywhere else.

"My name is Tim," he says in a rolling Dutch accent. "I am not a teacher but for the next ten days I will try my best to be your meditation instructor."

His eyes sparkle and I like him right away.

He wastes no time guiding us slowly, gently through the steps of *shamatha* meditation. This is the practice of mindfulness that I have been playing with for the past year and I feel the pride swelling again as I recognize the posture and method he describes.

"Sit with back straight and legs crossed," he begins. "Rest your hands in your lap, palms up, cradling each other with the left hand on bottom, right on top, thumbs barely touching. Relax your jaw and place your tongue on the roof of your mouth so you are breathing through your nose. Keep your eyes slightly open, gazing downwards..."

He speaks slowly. There is no rush to be anywhere or do anything.

"Now simply rest your attention lightly on the natural rhythm of your breath. Thoughts will come up. Sounds will come up. Sensations will come up. Don't worry. Just notice all of these things and gently bring your awareness back to the breath."

He rings the little bell in front of him and now forty-eight people sit quietly and unmoving, some for the first time in their lives. But this is not my first time. I sit with confidence, knowing what lies ahead.

So I settle in, wrap my knees in my warm wool shawl. I breathe in and out. My thoughts buzz and flutter. I am in India! I am on retreat! I have made it! But I take another inhale and just like I learned back home, I come back to the breath. Then the whole world takes a long, easy breath with me and is for a moment very, very still.

Five minutes pass and I realize that already my thoughts have drifted, though I don't know when or how. Just when I am about to remember what I am doing, sitting here amongst a group of strangers, I notice the breath of my neighbor. It is a thin, high-pitched whistle through his right nostril. I smile knowingly to myself. Then I bring my attention back to my own breathing.

Eight minutes pass and the whole group moves like a slow, sloshing wave from one side of the hall to the other. Joints creak and crack as people shift on their cushions. But I do not move. I will not move. I have meditated *fifteen* minutes a day for the past twelve months and so I continue to sit with ease as I come back to the breath.

Twelve minutes. A cough, a sneeze, a sigh. I notice all of these and gently return once more to the breath.

But then, at sixteen minutes, I notice a burning, searing pain in my knees. Drops of sweat gather on my temples and one by one begin the slow descent down the sides of my face. Heat is poured on top of heat and soon there are no thoughts, no breathing neighbor, no silence, no cushion, no India, no meditation hall. There is even no breath now, only the ringing in my ears and the grinding of my teeth as I imagine someone driving long, sharp spikes into my kneecaps. I grab them, knead them, rub them. I rock and roll and shut my eyes tight.

Finally I let out a little gasp. I give in. I quietly uncross my legs and wait for relief. But there is no relief. The pain continues even worse than before and for the next twenty-three minutes I am Agony and Despair. Visions of nine more days of torturous sitting just like this consume me. I am not going to make it.

Tim finally rings the bell, long after I had given up any hope of ever hearing it again. We all groan together and I think we all want to cry.

Tim has not moved. Not one inch. His legs are still twisted up in the half lotus position, one ankle resting on the opposite thigh. He is comfortable, serene, even refreshed after forty minutes of sitting. He smiles at us now. He has seen all this fear, doubt and frustration before.

"It's not too easy is it?" he says. "Don't worry. Be patient. This practice is not to be mastered in a day or a few weeks. After twenty years you may find that your ability to concentrate has improved. That's all for tonight. Get a good nights rest and remember: cherish the silence."

We all file out of the gompa now, feet shuffling and scuffling into the dark Indian night. The quiet of the pine jungle around us seems forbidding now. I think I have made a mistake by coming here and as I look into the eyes of those around me, I know they are thinking that too.

We head to our rooms, one by one. We do not say goodnight. We do not say anything at all. We just awkwardly crawl under the covers, each with three people around us we have never met, and turn off the lights.

In my dream a figure in robes is walking along a winding stone path through the mists and the trees. It is a still moment, a perfect moment, and I think that the sun has just stretched his arms up over the unseen horizon. Out of this peace and silence I can hear the ringing of a great bell. It fills all of space, and it is pure and high and clear.

"What a wonderful way to wake up," I think as the figure in robes comes closer.

The bell rings again, louder this time. I roll over out of sleep and pick up my watch.

6:06 it reads.

"Oh shit, oh shit, oh shit, oh shit!" I cry as I snap up out of bed, knocking my head on the shelf above. The stone Buddha tumbles down into my lap but I do not see that he is smiling at me all the while. I put him back on the shelf, leap out of my sleeping bag and in one fluid motion I am in my shoes and heading for the door. My roommates stir out of their own dreams and try to focus through sleep-filled eyes. But I am already gone out into the mists and blue light of the real dawn.

I run down the slippery, moss-covered steps, straining my ears for the next ring of the bell. I come around the corner and there is John walking up the path towards me. His hair is tousled and he is still half asleep.

"Sorry, sorry," I say breaking the silence again. I wince, waiting for some stern word or rebuke. But he doesn't scold me or shush me or slap my wrist. He just hands me the gong and with a nod and a sleepy smile walks back down the path.

I stand still for a moment and laugh under my breath. It is so quiet up here in these hills. The only noise I can hear is the noise inside my head. But even that fades away as I take the gong and the mallet up to the last spot of the morning's rounds. I stand there on the top of the hill overlooking the gardens and the gompa. I hold the bell high, swing the mallet. Then I wait and listen as the silence holds the ringing close in her arms like a mother who has called her one and only child home.

Chapter 6

First Love Revisited

Hey lover! It's me again.

Do you remember the second time I saw you? It was years after we had parted and three thousand miles away from that time and place you let go of my hand and gently nudged me into my long hiding. You had changed your body and your name, but still, that didn't fool me. I know, I know. This sounds crazy. But I swear to you it's not. It *was* you, I'm sure of it.

You had become so beautiful then with long bleach-blonde hair and tight rocker boy jeans, strutting up and down the halls of Laguna High with your retinue of nymphs and dryads surrounding you like some flirtatious, golden Pan. I tried so hard not to stare but I couldn't take my eyes off of you.

In a way, you were too beautiful, too cool and I thought, *no wonder he doesn't remember me*. Day after day I would slink down the hill to the prison of home and languish away in the knowledge that you didn't recognize me at all, that you didn't even know I was alive. At best I was just some east coast hick with tangled red hair and pale skin that glowed like some weird lichen in the southern California sun. There was no way you would ever have anything to do with me.

And so, day after day, I stood on the corner with all the other outsiders, all the rockers and punks and left-behinds, and watched you and all the other beautiful people pass by. We'd sneer at you, resentful and jealous, feeling cheated and left out from the rest of the world as we smoked cigarettes and thin joints and tried so hard to look tough and cool.

"Hey, nice shirt," you said one day as you slowed down in your yellow Porsche 911.

We all stood there in awe, forgetting the rule of cool for a split second, letting our jaws drop down to the sidewalk as I spun around bewildered to see who you were talking to. I looked down, saw my ripped Ronnie James Dio t-shirt, faded and black, and realized you were talking to me. Then you winked as you stepped on the gas and those fat tires left thick chunks of burning rubber sticking to the asphalt like breadcrumbs, all the way up the hill, all the way up to paradise.

I skipped down the hill that day, smiling for the first time in a year, like a whistling rainbow in the dark, down and away from the castles and palaces that sprawled across the hillside above. You had noticed me! I *was* alive!

Do you remember the next day when you slowed down by Stoner's Corner and told me to hop in? It was like a waking dream! I slid into those black leather seats, hot and sticky from the sun and off we went to the Taco Bell. You cranked up Ozzie's Crazy Train and we wailed out the chorus to the clear blue sky and rocked out the solos on our air guitars.

"You should come over sometime," you said. "We can jam."

My heart leapt into the air before it dove off the side of the coast highway over the cliff and into the sea. I didn't even have a guitar.

But that night at home I blurted it out anyway. "A-kid-from-my-class-wants-to-know-if-I-can-come-over-this-Saturday-to-play-guitars-and-just-hang-out."

I winced as my mom and the Lord looked at each other then back at me through narrowed eyes. They probed me with questions about you, where you came from, what you looked like, what kind of clothes you wore. They frowned and crossed their arms when I told them about your car and I gave up any hope of ever seeing you again. Then I waited in the stifling silence while they transferred thoughts from mind to mind.

"OK," they said finally and I didn't question the mystery of it at all as I slipped off to bed.

When Saturday came I couldn't get away from home fast

enough. I went down to the beach to meet you two hours early. The morning fog wrapped around my skin and by the time you pulled up, I was wet and shivering in the chill of Southern California December.

We sped up into the hills and I forgot all about the cold as I watched in awe as the mansions whooshed by. Pretty soon I lost count of all the Mercedes and Jaguars and Bentleys, of the wide patios with tall glass windows overlooking the Pacific, of the hot tubs and swimming pools of azure, of the sculpted jungle gardens of the homes of the gods.

By the time we came to your house my head was spinning. I looked over at you and I knew, plain and simple, that I was in love. We went inside and your mother shouted to us from the kitchen. She was tan and golden just like you, dressed in a flowing silk pool dress of turquoise and paisley. Her fingers were heavy with fat, sparkling gemstones. She called herself a Lady of Leisure and threw her head back in a rolling laugh as she poured us lemonade and sent us off to your room to play guitar.

I sat on the side of your bed, watched you sling on that cherry red Kramer Flying V, switch on your amp with a screech of feedback and tear into the intro of Crazy Train. My mouth dropped open. You were so good!

By the time you handed the guitar over to me I had forgotten the three chords I knew. I held it there in my hands while the amp groaned and hummed impatiently, waiting for me to do something, anything. I fumbled around the neck but my fingers didn't know what to do on the narrow little fret board. All I could get out of it was a muddled mess of distortion and feedback. Then I handed the instrument back to you, defeated, and shook my head.

I came over again the next weekend. Then the next. The routine was always the same. I would watch you play with my chin in my hands and my eyes filled with love and lust. You'd let me play until neither one of us could stand it anymore then we'd listen to your records for hours. All the while we squirmed in the stew of hormones that boiled around us. Sometimes I'd catch your nervous sidelong glances and I knew what you were thinking. Did you know what I was thinking too? Either way, neither one of us had the guts to do anything about it.

Until that one day when you finally did. You had picked me up from our rendezvous point at the beach, and we drove in silence all the way to your driveway. I looked down at your bronze legs in your short shorts, swooning in a rush of heat and blood.

"So, what do you want to do today?" you said as you shut off the engine.

It was the question of the month, of the year, of my life but I just shrugged my shoulders.

"Well," you said with a coy yawn and stretch of your arms. "No one's home so...we could just go inside and beef each other."

The sky opened up, music poured from the clouds above, my heart leapt into my throat and I burned with the thrill of the promise of sex. I felt your eyes on me, waiting for my answer, waiting for any sign of approval, rejection or even disgust.

"Yes, yes, yes!" I cried in my mind. But I wasn't quick enough and before I could form the words on my lips and push them out, you started to laugh. I waited, with the *yes* that would have changed the world ready to leap off the end of my tongue.

"Just kidding," you said. "Me and my friends at my old school used to joke like that all the time. Pretty funny, huh?"

Then you opened the door to your car and left me sitting there in sad and silent disbelief. We were so close, so ready to put aside all the confusion and doubt, to embrace who we were, who we could have been, to put to rest all the questions of *am I* or *aren't I* or *who am I?* Then you shut the door and all I could do was watch as you walked away and up the stairs.

One day the Lord came to pick me up from your house. It was the first time he had ever met you. You stood there in the doorway with the sun shining on your long, blond hair and your short shorts. He looked you up and down with a sneer and a fake smile that barely contained his contempt. But you just went on smiling and so I smiled back too wishing that I could just reach out and hold your hand, right there in front of him, proud and defiant. When we got in the car my stepdad didn't say a word for the whole drive home, he just stared straight ahead and never once looked at me.

"I don't think it's a good idea to spend any more time with that boy," my mom said that night.

"Why?" I asked.

"Well, Daniel thinks he's gay."

I wanted to laugh and dance and cry all at once. I knew it! You *were* gay! How could I have ever doubted it? But then I started to tremble and shake as I realized that once again it was me that was being accused of that nameless crime.

I stomped my feet, ran to my room and slammed the door. I cranked up the stereo and screamed. I belted out the lyrics to all my songs of frustration and rage. My fists pumped in the air to the angry rhythm. I dove off my bed and bounced off the walls. I spun and twirled till I fell sweating and panting to the floor.

I laid there for a while till my head rolled off to one side and saw the wall behind my door. It was my secret shrine to my gods of rebellion, but now I saw that the posters of my rock 'n roll heroes, snarling and sexy in tight leather pants, were all torn down. I remembered the ransacking of my room two years before and thought, *oh god, it's happening again.*

Late that night I was ripped out of sleep by a violent shaking and a bright light in my eyes. My blood pumped full of fear. There was the Lord shining a flashlight into my face and gripping me tight by the arm. He was seething and spitting and so close that I could feel his hot breath stinking of cigarettes.

"Who do you think you are?" he hissed.

I was so frozen with fear that I didn't even understand the

question.

"Making your mother see that smut you hang up on your walls. You wanna look at pictures of men with cocks sticking out of their pants, you do it when you're on your own, you got that?"

He pushed himself off of me like a trampoline, pinning my shoulder hard against the mattress as he stormed out of the room, slamming the door behind him, leaving me to shiver there in the dark, scared and numb.

I didn't see you for months after that. The best I could do was to hang out at our old spot where you used to pick me up and sit on the splintered old bench. It was there that I saw you finally in the middle of the summer. Even though you were far away, I could see *her* hanging on your shoulder and you were making her laugh while she playfully punched you in the arm.

I sat on the bench for a long time. There were no tears, no feeling at all, just the crash of the waves and the wind and the seagulls hovering above. As you got closer I shut my eyes tight and prayed. I prayed to become invisible, prayed that I would disappear, prayed that you would never see me again. I chanted those little mantras over and over until I felt myself growing light and translucent. The wind picked up and it seemed like it was lifting me up into the air, inland and over the mountains like the morning fog. When I finally opened my eyes I saw that you had already passed. The magic had worked. I was no one. I had melted into thin air.

Chapter 7

True Believers

Listen to me now. You are fifteen years old. You are gay but you don't want to believe it. You don't want to believe it so bad that you push it deep, deep down into the dark center of your heart so that even you forget where you put it. Even when it rears its ugly head in fantasies that come unbidden in the night, you just plug your fingers in your ears and shut your eyes tight.

"La, la, la, la, la," you silently scream. But no one is listening anyway.

Then you can't sleep at all so you sneak out of the house to drink beers and smoke pot with your other lost friends. You get high and drunk until you are numb, until you forget your name, your life, your dreams. But at least it makes you a little bit happy. Doesn't it?

Now imagine that you don't have any gay friends at all, that you have no one to look to and say: *Yes, that's me; that's got to be me.* Instead the only gay boy you know is too pretty, too soft, too feminine and the other kids at school hiss at him through gnashing teeth and foaming lips.

"Faggot!" they say. "Fucking faggot!"

No, that's not you. Not in a million years. That's not you...is it?

But even when you sneak into your friend's mother's closets, pull out the prettiest silk and lace and dance around free for those few seconds that are like a dream, you are still trapped in the cage of denial. You come and then recoil in terror as you see the broken little bird writhing on the floor there in the tall mirror that never lies. And then a knock on the door and a stifled *oh my god*...

Now on top of that, under that, through that imagine that you come home from school everyday, to the cult of home. You shut the door behind you and there is the Lord, ever ranting and raving, jabbing his finger at the Book, pointing with a growing fever to the proof of the Word. But it is not the word of God alone. It is the word of all gods. A crazy, clamoring confluence of words. Crystals and auras and chakra yoga. Time travel and the end of the world. Fruit fasts and the cleansing of your impure soul. Pyramid power and perpetual motion. Telekinesis, astral projection, mediums and magical thinking. Reincarnation and disembodied ghosts. Human potential and positive thinking. Conspiracies. Conjectures. Paranoia.

"Now I know everything!" cries the Lord again and again. "Now we can truly believe!"

And so you follow the Lord and the Mother, starry eyed now, down this thorny path of disbelief. It is a long, dusty pilgrimage to nowhere and along the way there are New Age carnivals and vision quests, Hare Krishnas and spiritual tests. There are lunatics and visionaries, witches and saints and every one of them beckons you to follow down dark alleys and secret stairs. You follow until your head spins. You follow until you can't tell right from wrong, up from down, black from white. But always there are signs and portents leading the way. They hide in every number, every shadow, every word and the Mother and the Lord read them like bones.

"It's ok," they say in unison. "We know the way. We are on a Mission from God."

But God works in mysterious ways and one day he comes to the Lord and tells him to read a New Book and it explodes in your lives like a volcano. At first it is all heat and light and wonder. This is what it has all come to. This is, finally and without a doubt, the Truth.

So the Lord baptizes you all in the new faith. He shows you the error of your ways. He teaches you the new mantras and the new prayers. He wakes you in the still of the night, in the dark, shaking you out of sleep to make sure that you're dreaming the words. He cleanses and purifies, goes away on long retreats. Sometimes you even think (or is it hope?) that he might be gone forever. But always he returns.

Then one day he is standing in the doorway, a half-mad Moses, eyes shining with a terrible light. It is time to follow once more. Time to be brought before the Elders, time to be judged and finally saved. You shudder and shake. Will you be found worthy?

And so he takes you all to the Great Temple and everywhere is the face of the one true Prophet. His cold, blue eyes stare from every wall and they see all of your secrets. Everywhere His words are written in gold and the sound of His voice echoes through time and space. And even though He is dead and gone now for twenty years the true believers wait with open arms for his return.

Here at this great gathering of the faithful you all revel together in your new salvation and clarity. With glassy eyes and plastic smiles you chant and sing the Doctrine, the Method and the Way.

"This is the way to happiness!" you all cry. "This is the way to freedom!"

At first you just mouth the words but then you are forced to learn the melody of freedom and the others correct you with wrinkled scowls when you sing a little out of tune. All day you sing and dance for them as they clap in time. All day you perform with no food or rest.

Finally, when you are delirious with hunger and thirst and half asleep they take you to the High Priestess. She looks you and your brother and the Mother through and through. Yes, you are ready. You will do.

"Well, are you ready to be Free?" she asks.

You look to the Mother for some sign or cue but she is paralyzed by the powerful spell of the High Priestess' gaze and doesn't blink or move. You look to your brother as he shivers now, silent and scared. You look to the Lord, who stands behind you with bloodshot eyes, hanging on every word.

"Sure," you say with a shrug and a voice that's not your own.

And then the High Priestess claps her hands as she throws back her head and laughs.

"Good, good!" she cackles and cries.

And just like that your fate is decided. You will swell the ranks of the faithful. You will leave the world of confusion behind. You will be purified and set free. There will be no need for schools, or family, or jobs, or friends. You will have new friends now and a bigger family who will teach you and guide you along the True Way.

"Bring the children this way," the High Priestess says to the Mother. "We will take it from here."

But the High Priestess, swollen with arrogance, has spoken too eagerly, too greedily and now the spell is suddenly broken. You look over to your right and there is your mother, your real mother who you thought was lost, returned to sanity for just a moment.

"You're not taking my children," she cries. And with panic in her eyes she grabs you both and carries you out into the hall. You fly on tiptoe with the High Priestess chasing you down. You fly for your lives. You fly into the golden light of the setting of the sun, to the car, to the highway, to home.

And so your mother has saved you in the end. But it is too late. You sit in silence with your brother still shivering next to you in the back seat. You stare at the back of the head of the Lord that now hangs in shame. You look into the eyes of the Mother in the little mirror that never lies. No one speaks. No one is sure what has just happened. But you know.

You speed along the highway now. The window is open just a crack. The air blows into your eyes so they sting and burn from the smog and the heat. They are dry and red but you do not blink.

For the first time in your young life you are seeing things clearly and though they are terrible and merciless, you cannot take your eyes away. *This is the end of trust,* you think. *This is the end of faith.* And there in the silence, you promise yourself that you will never believe in anything ever again.

Chapter 8

The Teachings

Believe nothing, no matter where you read it, or who said it, no matter if I have said it, unless it agrees with your own reason and your own common sense. ~ The Buddha

Venerable Jampa Dekyi faces the altar in the gompa at Tushita and there is no doubt, no fear and no shame in her eyes as she bows. Before her is the massive golden statue of the Tibetan saint, Tsongkhapa. He looks down at us with wide eyes that stare out from the illumination we have all come here to taste. He is adorned in saffron silk robes and offerings of snapdragons, apples, incense and chocolates, all the bounties of this life, have been lovingly scattered around him. Other Buddhas hang in the form of *thanka* paintings on the high walls and I try to pick them out from my studies. My tongue gets twisted in knots as I sound out the strange Sanskrit names to myself: Maitreya, Avalokiteshvara, Manjushri, Vajrasattva. I watch and wait as the nun prostrates herself to all of these, laying her body out full length and flat on the floor three times before taking her seat.

Oh how the sight fills me with awe and admiration! To believe! I mean truly believe! Twenty years now running away from faith and belief, trapped inside in the Temple of Me, following the rites and insane rituals of the Doctrine and the Church of Me. Where did it ever lead me? To more and more suffering. To hopelessness. To the needless punishment of myself and everyone around me.

But today I stand apart from the rest of the group. Today I am not merely a seeker. I am a Buddhist now. And though I am still uncertain, still kneading the tough heart of disbelief that stands on the edge of the great commitment, I am almost ready.

So when the teacher finally sits I begin my own bows. I bow to her with all the reverence I can muster, as if she were the Buddha himself manifest here before me now. I bow to the words she is about to speak, the Dharma, the teachings that lead to liberation. I bow to the Sangha, the community of those who have followed the words and attained the ultimate freedom from suffering for themselves. I bow with all my faults and short-comings of the past, present and future, held out as an offering in my open hands. I bow for every unkind word I have ever spoken, for every piece of bread I ever stole, for every time I betrayed myself, abandoned myself, gave up on myself. Yet through all of this I bow without a trace of self-pity or loathing. I am simply me, faults and all, and that is good enough.

When I take my seat again I am filled with gratitude. I am here! I am alive! How many times did I wish for my heart to simply stop beating? How many times did I try to step into that great void? Too many.

But now I look up at the nun and the *thankas* and all the students sitting around me furiously taking down notes and trying so hard to understand. We are *all* trying so hard to under-stand. Suddenly I don't mind the pain in my knees as much any more. The boredom gives way to a growing joy and I think that this would be a good way to spend a part of my life. To sit and quietly listen for a change. To devote myself to learning as much as I can. To slough off the arrogance and false pride of the addict and finally concede to the possibility that someone else might just have a few of the answers.

"When did your mind begin?" the nun asks. She smiles at us now the smile of an old Australian grandmother as her eyes sparkle through thick rimmed glasses. There is not a trace of arrogance behind them, only certainty. She has asked the question of herself many times before. She has spent long days and nights searching for the beginning of the mind and after shining the bright light of concentration on it has discovered that each moment of mind depends on a similar, previous moment. Tracing back the cause, she has found that our minds stretch far back into inconceivable, beginningless time.

I follow the line of reasoning myself, checking my own experience. I stretch my memories back as far as I can. Then, when I can't remember anymore, I let my imagination take over. I go all the way back to the darkness and heat of the womb, all the way to the point of conception. But there, I stop. Where was my mind before that? What caused it to be in the first place? Was it the coming together of sperm and egg? Or did it just spring out of nowhere without any cause at all?

"Our minds are beginningless," she says still smiling. "Our mind streams continue on and on, taking new rebirths again and again. In fact we have been born countless times in countless different forms."

And so the old nun tells us a story with no beginning or end. She tells us the story of our minds, confused and deluded, grasping at phantoms and ghosts and things that were never even there. She tells us how we cling to a self that we believe is real. We cater to its endless desires; indulge all its petty whims. What's more, we believe that this self is the *body* we inhabit. We cherish it and protect it and serve it with every ounce of energy we have. But then, without warning or notice, the body dies leaving the mind untethered and afraid. Desperate, we search for another body to be born into and in our great fear, it doesn't matter what kind of body it is. It could be an animal, an insect, a fish. All we care about is finding some solid, permanent place where we can feel safe again and rest.

But there is no rest here in *samsara*, this endless wheel of cyclic existence. Instead we wander eon after eon feeling alone and lost, thinking we are unique and separate, thinking that we are the only ones who suffer, that we are the only ones who truly matter.

"I want you all to imagine something now," Jampa Dekyi says. "Just assume for a moment that all of this is true, that you have been born countless times before. Let us also assume that there are countless beings in countless universes who have also been born countless times. If all of this is true then it stands to reason that each and every one of those sentient beings has been your mother an infinite number of times."

This is the vast view of Buddhism and our minds collectively explode.

"Now let us meditate on the kindness of your mother in this life," she says.

My teeth start to grind until I wonder when they will crack and shatter. My muscles tense. I thought I made peace with my mother before I came here. I thought I forgave her and asked for her forgiveness. I thought I had already sifted through the rubble of the past and found a new foundation to build on. But here, in India, ten thousand miles away, I find that all of that brick and mortar has not yet set.

So cautiously I meditate on the kindness of my mother taking careful, unsure steps into this old house. At first, it's like poking the hornets' nest of all my anger and resentment. Kindness? Mother? For years I never put those two words in the same sentence. It was my mother who was to blame for all the tragedy of my life and I had laid that blame squarely at her feet for years. She was not a source of comfort to me, but the cause all my suffering. *She* was the one who had made me hate myself. *She* was the one who made me ashamed for being gay. *She* was the reason I drank and got high and wanted to die. If only she had tried harder to understand. If only she had...

But I stop myself and return to the sound of the nun's steady voice.

"Try to imagine the sacrifices your mother made for you all the way from the time you were conceived," she says.

So here, I stop resisting. I stop playing the old loop that's been droning on for so many years. I go back in my mind, trying to imagine what it would have been like: the sickness, the weight gain, the discomfort. I imagine her, night after night, trying to turn herself over in bed, unable to get comfortable. I imagine the kicking and the turning, the prodding and poking of the life inside of her. Then I try to imagine the pain of childbirth itself and though I come up short, I begin to understand a little. At least I know what pain is and I realize that I have never really endured it willingly for someone else. I imagine all the sleepless nights my mother experienced after my birth, how she got up whenever I cried, without hesitation or thought for herself. Then I remember that there was always food on the table and a warm, dry place to sleep. I remember her defending me against bullies and Irish setters, risking her reputation and even lying for me to protect me. Even when I rebelled against her and tried so hard to hurt her as a way to call attention to my pain, she still loved me and to the best of her ability and wisdom gave me all the care and support that she could. At the very least, no matter what her faults, no matter what mistakes she made, I am here right now mostly because of her.

"Now generate the wish to repay that kindness," Jampa Dekyi says. "Even if you think it would take your whole life to do so, make that sincere wish."

It is a tall order but I try anyway.

"Now," the nun says. "Let go of all the limitations you think you have and apply that feeling to all beings, remembering that every one of them, every human being, every fish in all the oceans, every bird in the sky, every frog and every insect, has shown you infinite kindness throughout your beginningless lives."

My heart opens and a little bit of light begins to creep in. I imagine the presence of all those limitless sentient beings around me, all my kind mothers of the past, present and future, all of them suffering in their own way. They don't seem so much like disembodied strangers anymore and just by admitting this to myself, that there are others out there besides me, I feel a huge relief. *Here is the purpose I have been seeking in a purposeless life!* Here is the potential to be of help to others who are suffering just like me, who want happiness just like me. And what's more, Buddhism claims to show me how to live this way.

The meditation comes to an end. We untwist our legs, massaging the knotted muscles and joints. As I look around, I see that everyone's faces are glowing with crescent smiles and faraway looks and with a quiet, little laugh I realize that I am not so unique or alone after all.

Chapter 9

Wandering

My neighbor showed me his hard on through his sweats today but at seventeen years old I still didn't have the courage to reach for it, even with trembling fingers. He looked at me with a wink and how-do-you-do but I just shied away pretending it wasn't there. Instead I took another sip of beer, another hit off the joint, another drag off my cigarette. Three little lies that I told myself to help me forget the embarrassment, the longing and the shame. Then he just shrugged his shoulders and was gone.

So now I am home, drunk and stoned. I wobble a little two-step by the kitchen sink as I help with the dishes after dinner. The little wisps of steam dance in front of me and I laugh as I reach out to grab them.

My mother stands next to me and as I hand her the hot, wet plates I can feel her staring eyes cutting into me. She leans in close, catches the scent of booze on my breath.

"Have you been drinking?" she asks as the tears gather like dark clouds. But it is still the wrong question. *Yes your faggot son is drunk* is what I really want to say, already so good at calling myself names.

"Yes," I answer instead with chest stuck out in my newfound, contrived bravado. I tell myself I don't care what she says or does anymore. I am tired of all the hiding and the lies, tired of sneaking around in the dark, tired of playing this leading role day after day and night after night.

The dismay in her eyes washes me away in great waves of WHAT-IS-WRONG-WITH-YOU? and WE-JUST-DON'T-KNOW-WHAT-TO-DO-WITH-YOU. It sends me head over heels, tumbling down a stony riverbed and I smash and break against the boulders of her disappointment.

Yes, there *is* something wrong with me. Yes, I need to be fixed.

"We can't take it anymore," she finally says and now the weight of this moment is an unstoppable, moving monolith of stone. I plant my feet on the hard, slippery earth, try to heave it back up the hill of time but it pushes me ever forward into the fixed and unchangeable future that opens up like wide and hungry mouth.

"We think it's time we send you back to live with your father," she says finally and then the future swallows me whole right then and there.

I go to my room, pretend to pack, but I leap out the side window instead, down the old drainpipe slick with algae and slime. I slip into the street and run light footed and half-free through the shadows and the shade. I run all the way up the coast, five miles in the dark as the violent ocean cheers me on. I run to my only friend's house and knock on the door.

"Sure, my Dad will let you stay here," he says on behalf of his Dad who is never there. And then we throw a little party and get drunk to celebrate my long awaited escape.

No more cults! No more paranoia! No more lunatic mission from God!

Two months to graduation. I will make it, I say. I will go on to college. Far from the madness and the noise of home I will find out who I really am. I will make something of myself. And then they'll see...

When the morning comes I go to school with my head held high. I find my seat in the classroom, pull out my notebook and pen. This is too easy, I think. I should have run away years ago.

I look up from my desk. The police are outside the door now. They have come for me. There is nowhere to run. They take me by each arm and their walkie-talkies crackle and hiss, breaking the silence of our long march down the high school halls. The heads of two thousand classmates I never knew whip around to watch me pass. Then, as the police escort me out into the bright sun, two thousand sets of eyes stare out the windows as they push me, naked and exposed, into my mother's car.

No one says a word on the way to the airport. There are no explanations or final goodbyes. There are no tears either as we drive through the canyon, out to the highway and all I can do is stare in disbelief as the cactus and the sage and the coyotes fly by.

I am back in Connecticut. It is spring. It is 1988. Next week is graduation. Soon I will be out on my own but not in the way I imagined.

The letter rests next to the bowl of fresh fruit on the table. I pick it up and it is heavy with the juice and nectar of possibility. I think it even smells sweet as I bring it to my nose, taking in a great breath of its sweetness. I hold it in my shaking hands for a long while, though gently, like a precious newborn. My Dad makes pass after pass outside the kitchen window and the scent of fresh cut grass and gasoline waft through the fluttering lace curtains. It smells a little like hope as I tear the envelope open.

I have been home for a month now. But the deep old forests I used to play in don't remind me of home anymore. They surround me now with too much green, too much teeming, squirming and chomping life. The locusts and cicada rattling and buzzing their mad little tune outside my window have forgotten the lullaby that used to send me to sleep on sticky summer nights. Even the faint smell of ocean up there on the high wind doesn't fill me with nostalgia.

Where is home now? Where do I belong? I spend my nights and days longing for California but even that doesn't seem like home anymore.

I unfold the letter and read:

Dear Christopher,
We are pleased to inform you that you have been accepted for enrollment at California State University...

A wide land opens up in my mind and the rolling plains and sharp peaked mountains stretch all the way back to the Pacific. I spin and twirl on tiptoes, lifting my arms up high in a victory dance. I will go back to California after all! I will return on my own with pride and purpose. I will move into a little dorm room with nothing but a box of books and a reading lamp. I will get a part time job in the bookstore, take more classes than I can handle, drink too much coffee and smoke too many cigarettes as I cram for finals. I will make friends and plans and dreams come true before I finally graduate and head off into my bountiful future.

"Dad! Dad!" I cry. "I got accepted! I got accepted!"

I wave the letter like a million-dollar bill in front of me as I run out into the yard to meet him. I just want him to feel my joy, to give me a hearty slap on the shoulder and say, "Good job, son! You did it!" But instead he just lets the mower sputter and die as he takes the letter in calloused hands. He reads it slowly with a furrowed, sweating brow while he shoos away the mosquitoes and horse flies. It is quiet for a long time and I kick at a clod of wet grass that stains the tips of my sneakers with a black and slimy green.

"Where's the money going to come from for this?" he finally asks.

I have no idea. I have never even thought about it. All I know is that there has to be a way. So I put up a short and valiant struggle. I throw up my arguments against taking the safe and sure road with plans and solutions and ways out. I will only need enough money to get there, I tell him. Then I will work and apply for loans. I will figure out a way. But all of my answers are just horse flies and mosquitoes and he wrinkles his nose as he swats each one down.

"Why don't you just stay here?" he says. "Get a good job with good benefits."

Finally, I break down. I give in too easily. The deep old forest closes in around me now, dark and unfriendly. No, there will be no school, no bountiful future. My Dad hands me back the letter. It is thin like rice paper now and as I crumple up my little dream to stuff it into my pocket, it dissolves and melts away in my sweaty hand.

Graduation comes and goes and I take the path well traveled. I follow my father's advice. I get a job doing man's work. I lift, I heave, I load, I dig. There are no gay men here in the lumberyard, out, proud and free. To the men who work here we are just *fruits, dandies* and *queers*.

"Whadaya queer?" the foreman sneers.

"Not me, sir," I say. "Did ya ever hear the one about the two fags in the coconut tree?" And so it goes as I learn to hide myself and hate myself ever more and more.

I learn to drink like a real man, too, out there in the hard, frozen field after work. We drink big bottles of schnapps and six packs of beer. We chain smoke cigarettes and long joints of cheap brown pot until we are stumbling and drunk and spinning in the snow and the cold. We all hate our lives and all of us hide out here from wives and mothers, fathers and children. We drink till we can't see straight, till we forget, till we puke big spots of steaming red and yellow in the field, in the snow. Then we drink a little more.

It goes on for days and weeks and months like this until one day my father calls me down from my room in the attic.

"I found this funny little reefer in your ashtray," he says.

He spins it around on the kitchen table in lazy revolutions with the half-smoked joint orbiting around in the groove on the side. There is no denying it now.

"I think you have a problem," he says. "I think it's time you moved out."

He is stern. He is unforgiving. He does not understand. I do not understand either. I do not see him twenty years from now, both of us different men, sitting quietly at the table talking deeply long after the lunch rush. I cannot see him reaching out his hand to me to gently squeeze mine. I cannot hear him say *I'm sorry and I love you no matter what*. So for today, all I can do is walk up the dark flight of steps to my room, pack my things and go.

I am eighteen, a man in the eyes of the world, out on my own now and I am tripping. I forget what we have taken. Synthetic mescaline. Yes, that's what they said it was. Little green gel caps that melted on our tongues and sing now in our young heads. Now it is cold and we are running fast through the woods and laughing, my roommates and I. Our voices echo through the old Connecticut forest and I think we are good friends and I'm so glad that we've found each other. We chase each other through the trees and I am whipped and cut as the branches slash my rosy cheeks. We pretend we are Indians and love this earth, our home.

But where are we? Where is home? Now I am lost. Where are the others? I am panicking on the inside but I don't show it. No one can ever know. No one can ever know. No one can ever know. So she finds me there in the dirt and the moss holding my knees like that, rocking back and forth. There, there she says and mistaking me for someone else, falls in love.

Soon the pendulum swings back and I am laughing again. We find the others, find my van and pile in. I have made some funny joke and everyone is back on my side, friends again to the end. Are you ok to drive? Sure, I say and I turn the key. I can drive on acid, I can drive on this. The road home is long so I stomp on the gas and try to aim straight, with everyone holding on and rolling like jelly beans in the back.

Stop here! Stop here! Stop here! My friend is shouting from the back seat so I brake hard and park. XXX neon shines from plywood-covered windows painted black. We enter at our own risk, sticking close as the world gets strange. Porn on mescaline is nothing like Dali. Bodies gleam glossy on slick paper and I pretend it's not sex, pretend I'm not turned on. We laugh and giggle like children holding hands as we sneak into the back to the peepshow booths and men in dark faces look away as we plunk our own quarters into the slots. Click through the channels and see it all for twenty-five cents. Every combination with a click, click, click. The other three laugh and laugh at the freak show called sex and when two men come on the screen, one of them taking the other hard and violent and furious, they squeal and point and cover their eyes. I try to look away too but I spread my fingers open instead, look deep into the screen and wonder how I can get to the other side.

But these friends, good as they are, won't give me directions. They don't know the way. I need a different map to a different country. But I can't find it anywhere so for now I am lost here, and alone. Soon it will be time to leave again, to wander again, without a map or a compass or even a destination.

Chapter 10

California

The sun rises behind me and the Pacific gleams like a hundred thousand sparkling, wish-fulfilling gems. I walk down the steps to the beach and baptize myself in the holy water. I am in California again but not in the proud and purposeful way that I hoped. Two years after high school I spent in the haze of acid and pot until I borrowed enough money from my best childhood friend to force an escape. He is with me now, slashed and bleeding from my betrayals and lies. I coerced the money out of him really, made it a condition of our friendship. Now he stands behind me, silent and seething.

But here I am now, starting a new life from the few dollars I have left from his kindness. It is enough to move into a house with four of his friends from the year before, onto a corner of living room floor and an egg foam mattress.

This little town is wild and on the tiny square mile cliff top overlooking the ocean I will try and fail to break free. But for now the place is beautiful to me and to the ten thousand college kids who call this their first home away from home. For us this is paradise. There are no rules, only youth unleashed. The days are lazy Southern California dreaming but at night the festival begins. Beer flows out of homemade kegerators, house parties go on for days and the air is filled with the endless jam of punk rock, funk and ska.

Drugs are everywhere.

When the weekend finally comes, the already deafening volume is just cranked up another notch. The streets are choked with a mass of drunken, swaying bodies until the chaos rises to a fevered pitch. By Saturday night we are dragging old couches into the street to set them on fire. We cheer and scream in the night as they blaze like sacrifices that light our faces red with the hunger for more and more and more of this new life. They burn to the ground. They burn until they are nothing but piles of the black ash of the pasts that we all want to forget.

My roommates throw dance parties of their own. Every weekend the call of P-Funk, James Brown and Sly is answered and before I have time to roll up my mattress there are two hundred people dancing across the living room floor.

We drink cheap beer, malt liquor and tequila and I think that I need it just to survive. I am still a self conscious and frightened little boy but when I pour the booze down his throat faster and faster he feels warm and free. He loosens up. He lets go. After ten beers he is passed out in the corner but I leap out reborn onto the dance floor in a twirling, whirling, flailing of limbs. The room erupts and everyone cheers and I become even drunker on the sweet fruit of their approval. And so I drink out of need, the need to be accepted, the need to feel right and normal in a world that I don't fit into. I drink as my sole purpose in life.

I read Bukowski, Kerouac and Burroughs and they become my new heroes. I want to be just like them so I write unintelligible poems and drink all day and night. Then I get up on the coffee table in the middle of the never-ending party and scream my mad verses to anyone who will listen. Sometimes I get a good laugh, sometimes I get punched in the face but mostly I just fall off my pedestal, vomit and black out.

So I slip and slide down this dangerous slope. I quit my job. I am drunk and obnoxious all the time. My roommates can't take it anymore and they finally kick me out. But I sneak back into the house to sleep when I think no one is home. Then they chase me away like a mangy coyote, wild and snarling. They throw stones at me until I leave the pack for good. I am homeless for weeks and sleep in the open fields or on the couches of strangers I meet at parties.

I get a new job, the only one I can find or even want, as the clerk at the all-night porn store. Every night I watch the parade of desperation march by. I can smell it in the sweat and semen of the slow trickle of men who amble in through the dark, cold mornings. They buy handfuls of quarter tokens from me and I plunk them into their hands like gold doubloons. They sink them into the video machines in the back, lock themselves in their dark closets until the electric-blue light of porn seeps out of the cracks in the doors. Then the air is filled with the soft moaning that becomes our subliminal mantra, calling us all to that which will never truly satisfy.

Sometimes I look at the baseball bat that leans under the cash register.

"Any 'a these fags tries to sneak into the booths together," my boss said. "Ya give 'em some of this."

But I can never do that. I can never even think of doing that so instead I turn a blind eye to the cameras pointed down peepshow alley and let them all do what they want. After all, I know what they're looking for back there in the dark, groping blindly and desperately, pressed against the sticky walls and tacky floors. And through the long nights I watch out of the corner of my eye and I'm never sure which is worse: the longing or the disgust.

I am spun on a little bump of speed that a regular gave me. He is a male prostitute and a heroin addict. He comes in high, after turning tricks in the parking lot and we kill the silent hours together. Sometimes he makes little passes at me but I always pull away.

"I just can't read you," he says and then he strokes my cheek.

But he is gone now and I am biting my nails until my fingers start to bleed when the phone jangles me out of my mind.

"Thank you for calling Downtown Books!"

There is nothing but silence on the other end and I am about to hang up when I hear a soft sobbing.

"Chris," says the voice I haven't heard in six months. "It's your Mom."

I remember the last time she called:

"The government has been infiltrated by a global communist conspiracy that wants to impose a new world order of godlessness on all of humanity and FDR knew this and so does the Pope and everyone is in on it and it's just that they've pulled the wool over our eyes and they put chemicals in our laundry soap that make us weak and compliant so I hope you aren't using laundry soap to wash your clothes and your step dad is a bible scholar now and we are out here in Colorado because God has brought us here to help save the planet from evil and I saw a movie the other day and there was a scene in it that was approaching Lesbianism and it made me so sick to my stomach that I almost threw up and I had to leave the theater..." she said.

Then I hung up the phone and vowed never to speak to her again.

Now I just want to smash the receiver on the counter top until it is pulverized into a thousand shards of my broken life. I want to scream into the mess of plastic and wire until she goes deaf from all my confusion and rage. I want to cut myself into little pieces and shove them one by one into the mashed little microphone so she can taste the blood of my failure.

But instead I meet her for breakfast in a rundown diner after work. I stare across the table at an apparition from some terrible dream. She is thin and pale and shaking. She is weak and sick and she looks like she is dying but when she looks up at me with dark hollow eyes, they still cut deep into me.

"I had a nightmare a few days ago," she says. "You were in a lot of pain and there were all these people around you. And they were *naked* and, and..."

I jab my fork into a piece of runny egg and shove it around my plate.

"Then I heard a voice as clear as yours or mine calling out to me: 'Your son, he needs help. You need to get out there right away!' So here I am!"

I can't bear to look at her. I know in my heart that if she knew the truth about me that she wouldn't be here at all.

But I play along. I pretend that I'm glad that she came. Yes, I need her help. I take her out into the beautiful day where the sun illuminates everything. I show her my life as it is. I show her the porn store and the fields that I sleep in. I take her to an afternoon keg party and get drunk and brag to her, while slouching over on a dirty curbside, about all the acid I've taken.

She bites her lip in fear and worry and I flash a devilish smile. Finally, I am winning. So I launch into a hundred thousand other war stories from the front lines of my addiction. I want her to see how far I've fallen, how helpless I've become. I want her to know that all of this is her fault. And from the curb I scream to her in my mind: Just ask the damn question!

But she still doesn't hear me, or doesn't want to. And for an hour, she just sits there next to me wringing her hands and holding back the tears.

I wake up hung over enough to not feel any shame. I poke my head from underneath the hotel blankets and see my mother zipping up her bags. Her bus back to Colorado leaves in an hour. I rub my eyes and groan.

"Ya know," she says. "You can always come home to live with us."

I throw off the covers and start to beat out the rhythm of a little tantrum.

"Ok, ok, I'm sorry," she says. "But will you at least quit that horrible job?"

"Mom, I can't just stop working."

Without saying a word she pulls an envelope out of her purse and sets it on the dresser.

"Don't open that till later and don't ever tell your stepfather about it."

We walk to the bus stop. The morning fog is just starting to burn off. We don't talk about the night before. We don't talk about anything at all. When the bus comes she reaches for me to give me a kiss and a hug but I pull away. I hand her her suitcase as she climbs up the steps while she looks down at me one more time. There are no more tears hiding in those eyes but I can see she is still sad.

As the bus pulls away I take the envelope out of my pocket. I unfold the slip of paper inside. It's a cashier's check for two thousand dollars. I read and reread the number again and again before I quietly fall apart.

Chapter 11

Suicide

Despair is the absolute extreme of self-love. It is reached when a man deliberately turns his back on all help from anyone else in order to taste the rotten luxury of knowing himself to be lost.

~ Thomas Merton

It's a cold, gray summer afternoon in San Francisco when I find myself standing outside of my body. I watch as my first wife paces back and forth at the end of the hall with a piece of white notebook paper in her hands. I had left it neatly folded on the bedside table for her to find when she came home from work. Now, hovering over her shoulder from above, I read the letter I've written and cringe. All those late nights sneaking off to North Beach, looking for men in some peep-show heaven were too much to admit, so instead I told her: *I am a porn addict and our relationship is a sham.* A few lines to make her hate me just enough to let me go. But that's not what I meant. It's not what I meant at all. I just wasn't ready to come out yet, not to her, not to myself.

So now I look down the hall and see my bag propped next to the front door. *Run, run, run,* I say to myself. Run from the pain of what is about to happen. Run from the truth. But something, maybe even courage, holds me to the ground under my feet. I have to see this through however cowardly I may feel.

Her hands start to shake like brittle leaves in a gathering gale and the paper falls out of her fingers, spiraling down to the warped hardwood floor.

"What the fuck is this?" she screams. "You bastard! You lying bastard!"

Our white German Shepherd scampers into the bedroom to hide, shaking under the bed. Then my wife tears off her wedding ring and throws it at me. The heavy silver band bounces off my chest with a dull *thunk* and hits the floor before rolling off under the kitchen table.

"Get out! Just get the fuck out of here! Get out, get out, get out!" comes the murderous crescendo and for a second I wonder why she doesn't try to stab me or strangle me or claw out my eyes. I back away, towards my bag and towards the door. She beats her fists on the walls, on the table, on her chest. Suddenly I feel nothing but regret for what I've done. All I wanted was to free us both from the lie I'd been living but instead I've broken her heart. So now I do run, down the steps and into the fog, tripping at the bottom into a full sprint. At the end of the street I hear her scream, full of blood and the end of the world, and that scream echoes inside my head for days.

"It's done. It's done. It's done. It's done," I chant to myself in between quick panic breaths that tear open my chest leaving my heart exposed to the chill and the wind. I put my head down and my feet flap hard and fast on the sidewalk as I head for nowhere at all. A bus pulls up, brakes screeching like nails on chalkboard and I get on without thinking. I find a seat and the city flies by stop by stop while I try to remember how I got here.

Six years together. Now gone, just like that. Three of them married. Some good years, some dark. But she was bright and sunshine and flowing dresses in Santa Barbara and as she shone on me I grew boundless for a while. I remember that first night in the beer garden as I saw her eyeing me nervously from the other table. Ten Meister Braus later I got up the courage to sweep her off her feet with a sneaky kiss and a smile. We ran all the way home to make love, my first time, and it was just so good to feel ok with another human being, to feel that embrace that I had only longed for and imagined.

And so not a night apart for more than I can count after that. Seven hundred happy sunsets at least, holding hands and laughing with heads tilted back in great guffaws of love.

Then a whisper one night in her ear: *I want to be with another man* and instead of pushing me out and away forever she pulled me in tighter and we both came, full of light, to the very thought it. So we danced through those hot sticky nights of summer searching until we found the one and he was perfect for the twenty minutes that three bodies needed to wrap themselves into one.

That night melted away through my fingers too fast and we didn't see him again for almost a year. I had almost forgotten him until there he was, another face in the party, holding hands with his lover, beaming proudly "Hey Chris. Hey, Sherry. I want you to meet my new *boyfriend!*" The word hung there in italics, sharp and serrated, and it cut my heart into two pieces until jealousy pumped out of them in hot, dark spurts. That could have been me. That *should* have been me.

There were other lovers after that and I wore my bisexuality like a second hand sweater, taking it off and putting it on when it suited me. But it was never enough and I tore myself apart inside all the time. Depression filled me up, depression I could taste like some thick black oil on my dry and swollen tongue. The days were all dark, one after the other without end, until the memory of sunshine and laughter disappeared into the void.

Then the meth came and everything unraveled: my life, my marriage and even the sweater.

Now, as I ride through San Francisco for hours, the city doesn't notice my nakedness at all. I am numb and shiver in the damp of dusk. I get off the bus and wander some more. There is nowhere to go. I reach into my wallet and count seventeen dollars in loose bills. She's frozen the accounts by now, a cold retribution.

Across the street a neon sign glows: Pharmacy with the mortar and pestle flashing hypnotically. The doors slide open and the air, thick with too much perfume of Dial and Pert Plus, tickles my nose. Is this what heaven smells like? I roam up and down the aisles pretending I don't have a plan, that I don't know exactly what I'm doing. I'm outside of my body again and I watch from above as I pick up little bottles one by one looking for that specific combination of letters and words that I will recognize only when I see them.

Then there they are. "In case of accidental overdose please call…"

I shake the bottle like a baby's rattle next to my ear. I shake it in a little rhythm, *shucka-shucka-shucka*, and walk it up to the counter in slow, shuffling steps. The clerk smiles at me through braces and acne as he rings me up.

"That'll be ten-seventy-eight!" he beams.

Outside, I find a payphone in the dark. The cars whiz by on streets slick with new rain and I let the plan simmer in the back of my mind letting the phone ring until he finally picks up.

My friend's place is small, a bedroom addition stuck haphazardly on the side of a rickety mustard yellow house in Potrero Hill. He gives me a big hug and looks me over like a mama bear inspecting her cub before I squeeze into his room. He didn't see this coming, fooled by the act I've put on for all these years. We drink beers and sniff little bumps of crystal as I try to explain what's going on. The burn and the rush fill me with hope and I forget for a little while the plan I have stuffed in my bag. I jabber on incoherently and we stay up all night until I start to think that my new life is going to be amazing.

"Are you gay?" my friend asks as my head snaps back from a line of meth.

The question stings more than the burning drug in my nostrils and I pretend at first not to hear it.

"Shauna thinks you might be gay," he says. She should know. Shauna who used to be Sean has a nose for these sorts of things.

"No! No!" I say with a shake and a wag and I look over my shoulder for the door, for the exit, for the great escape. But there's nowhere to run now. A parade of all my lovers tromps through the room with crashing cymbals and drums and trumpets and I worry that my friend can see them too. All the Chris's and Jimmies and Aarons and Mikes wave and shout as they walk by, "Hey Chris, don't you just love a parade?" I put my head down and pretend they're waving at someone else.

"No, not at all," I say.

My friend shrugs his shoulders and smiles like he knows something I don't know. The fanfare dies down as the parade turns down a dark alley. I smile back at him as I pass him the tray lined with rails of speed and he doesn't bring it up again.

The next day my friend goes to work and I am left alone with my thoughts. The euphoria of speed and beer are gone and I spiral down as the memories of the day before come back sharp and clear. They slash at me and though I put up my hands to fend them off they still cut deep. Phantoms and banshees swirl all around me calling me names. They check off long lists of faults and shortcomings cackling as they watch me squirm at the truth of them all. Liar, they say. Cheater. Betrayer. Pervert. Faggot.

I gasp and claw at the air begging them to stop. I fall over, curl up on the bed and tear at my hair until my scalp starts to bleed.

Then I remember the plan. I remember the pills and the darkness breaks just a little. I sit up and rub my eyes and for the first time in months I think I can see clearly what needs to be done.

I pull out my notebook and begin to write letters to all the people I love. The words drip onto the pages like a sweating fever. I write to my friend, to my brother, to my wife, to my mother, to my father. I apologize for all my failings and for all my broken promises. I tell them how I just can't bear to live one more day as a failed human being.

I am relentless and I don't even offer myself one tiny pinch of compassion. I am given over to the mind of suicide, selfish and beyond reason. All I see is my own pain and I don't care about anyone else or the consequences of my actions.

I fold the letters neatly, printing names in big letters on each one. Then I stack them on the bedside table propping them up so they won't be overlooked.

I find the bottle of pills and dump a pile of them into my hand. They look like little blue seeds and I begin to lay them out in front of me in neat little rows. I count out forty of them then pour myself a glass of water.

I pick up the first tiny blue pill and look at it between my fingers for a long time. I put it down then pick it back up again. Finally, I call my bluff and put it in my mouth, squeezing my eyes shut tight as I swallow. It is bitter and metallic as it slides down my throat and I resist the impulse to vomit as I take another one, then another. I take them faster and faster counting them out, "Twelve...thirteen...fourteen..." A life that might have been unfolds before my eyes. "Twenty-one...twenty-two...twenty-three..." A thousand possibilities of happiness, laughter and success rise up and fall away but they are nothing but mirages.

I lie down on the bed and fold my hands against my chest. As I close my eyes and wait, the chemicals work their way through my blood stream and I let go of my life. For a moment there is no impulse to fight or flee. I have given up. I am so tired and I let myself drift off to the very edge of sleep. It's very peaceful here with the cool breeze blowing in from the ocean, through the open window and across my face.

But suddenly my body jerks and heaves into a state of panic. What am I doing? Apparitions and ghosts of all the people I know and love have gathered around my bed. My brother, my mom, my dad, my friends, my wife. They all look so sad and for just a moment I am consumed by an unbearable empathy.

I twist off of the bed crying, "I'm sorry, I'm sorry, I'm sorry!"

I call 911.

"I've just taken forty sleeping pills," I say.

The operator is cool and unfazed. I give her the address and she sends me an ambulance like I'm calling for a Desoto Cab. Thank you and have a nice day, I think as I stumble out into the morning haze and fall down on the curb to wait for my ride.

Chapter 12

Meth

Devote the mind to confusion and we know only too well, if we're honest, that it will become a dark master of confusion, adept in its addictions, subtle and perversely supple in its slaveries.
~ Sogyal Rinpoche

May 11, 1998

I'm starting the pages again. I've neglected them for a while now. Can feel their lack. Haven't written a poem in a couple of weeks. Think I may be getting blocked up again without my emotional faucet. So much is going on in my life today. I'm dealing with it all pretty well though. Have felt really positive the past few days. Still, been doing lots of speed. Been using speed, pot and alcohol in my "ritualized" masturbation. I'm not sure if it's helping me cope with my sexual frustrations. Actually, I think it is. Just putting in disclaimers in anticipation of outside criticism. Does this make any sense? Just babbling. What do I want from all of this? Freedom. No responsibility for a while at least. Physical pleasure with no guilt or regrets. These are the things I was always denied growing up. Getting too hectic here—I don't want to go that deep right now. I've got to get going. The battery in the van is dead-have to tinker with it...

October 28, 1998:

Why have I been taking so many risks lately? Am I still suicidal? I worry that I am. The other night I took hit after hit off my glass pipe—I was seeking oblivion—mindless ecstasy no matter what the cost. It's not death that I seek but life. Life everlasting. Pure. The blood and guts. The stink of shit and sweat. Electric flesh. Laughter, agony and longing. The spirit and the flesh as one. Is that possible?

Is there any hope for me? I feel that if my eyes were opened even just a little to the hazy vision of my forgotten dreams I would blind the world with light. It's so hard to let go of my shackles. The traumas of my youth are still with me. My old hiding places still viable retreats. Been having anxiety dreams. One ended with mom appearing on a television. She wore too much make up. Her face was shining and plastic. She lectured me with plastic glee about responsibility. I woke up angry then became depressed and despondent. My past is not resolved. I have not forgiven. It's ok though. I will survive. I will be free.

January 12, 1999:

Yes, it's still morning. Spun. I can't bullshit my way through this anymore. Got to just admit it, all of it, the whole truth and I don't care who reads it. What are you reading my diary for anyway? Who gave you permission? Did I die a great man and this is now the fodder for fools to ponder and ah-ha? Well here it is. I am the greatest man who ever lived. Idol to millions. Worshipped like a god. When I speak there is a great hush. My words are the truth uncloaked. Because I am the fucking messiah! Don't you dare question me you pathetic little roach! How dare you doubt me even for a second. You're obviously not ready for my great teachings if you oppose me. Yes the messiah—I am the reincarnation of Christ, Buddha, Jim Morrison, Black Elk all the greatest men rolled into one. I am pure and strong and have nothing left to learn. My coming has been foretold. I am the one and only chosen one born now to save the world with my perfection and divinity. I believe this. I know this in my heart. I'm sure of it. All the signs, portents and coincidences say so. Mother said so...

May 21, 1999

Went to the porn store on Telegraph yesterday. Found an empty booth and left the door wide open. Then he came in and locked it behind him. I let him unzip my pants and I got hard and fierce *inside his mouth. I was shaking, up for days on the drug with no food or water. I came electric and all at once and it seemed like it would never stop. Then he spit me out onto the dirty floor and I got sick to my stomach. I weebled and wobbled and fell against the walls, reaching blindly to find a way out. I needed to get out of there but he kept trying to hold me and love me and keep me close. But instead I ran with him trailing behind me into the blinding sun. I ran without looking back. "I'll be ok, I'll be ok, I'll be ok..." I couldn't stop shaking and all I wanted to do was take it all back, to take back the come and the pleasure of it all and pretend it never happened.*

So I went out to the clubs and bought two rolls. Couldn't wait and took them in the cab only fifteen minutes from home. They hit me hard and fast in the backseat and the cabbie had to drag me out because I couldn't find my wallet or the door.

I took off all my clothes when I got inside and fell down on the floor, wrapping myself up like I was my own lover. Then I rocked myself back and forth and heard a voice as clear as the man standing inside my head.

"Chris, you're gay," he said and I realized the voice was mine.

I was so happy. I got up and danced naked and free for the only time in my life. I said it over and over again, out loud and unafraid of all the ears pressed against the walls. "Chris, you're gay, you're gay, you're gay!" Then I fell laughing back down to the floor and flirted with myself until I came down and fell asleep to the thought of finally throwing away all the drugs and learning how to live like a newborn in the morning sun.

But instead, I am awake now and it is the same old day. I got some more speed and I hate myself again. I hate myself for wanting him still. He sickens me: superficial, degrading, absurd emasculation. I am repulsed by his whimpering, feminine affectations.

Oh god! I'm just a pathetic piece of dogshit!!! Why do I feel this way? Why can't I be happy? I want to die! Loser! You suck I hate you I wish you would just die and stop being a burden. I wish you would go away. I wish you would take your weak pathetic helpless ass out of here and let me live!

July 19, 1999

Some bad things about speed:

I do it all the time.

Sometimes I get so high I forget to breathe.

I worry that everyone who sees me knows I'm spun.

My face turns red and my hands turn cold and purple.

My teeth are falling out and my breath smells a little like death.

It makes me crazy.

I don't take care of my dog.

It controls me. Sometimes I do it only hours after saying I wouldn't.

I don't even like it anymore.

It defines me and that's scary.

July 22, 1999:

Letting it all out. Brain frazzled. This is the part that holds me back. I hold myself back. I'm trying to love myself. This is gibberish. Like a madman walking and talking to know one. I want to quit speed once and for all. No more last times. I want to be a golden man, a man of the New Birth. How grand! Flip-flop. Can't make up my mind when I'm in this state of mind. Will this freak me out tomorrow or will I be able to laugh and love? I saw the sun rise earlier. Everything was clear. That wasn't the first time this morning or this year. I am changing but I cling to old habits, old thoughts, old tricks. I want to love myself. Really love myself. That means know myself. I am so close. My spirit is waking up (or is it?). I worry that I might be gay but I want to rejoice that part of me is gay. Trying to assimilate it all consciously. That is impossible. The method to achieve understanding is impossible to teach or describe. Yet it must be acted out precisely nonetheless. I know what I'm saying then sometimes I don't. I didn't mean for this diary to turn out like this today. But what else could it possibly be for? I sometimes just want to stop thinking. Stop the input, the incessant analysis of the same old data. Am I still in some kind of prison? Are there others like me? Yes! I've seen them with my own eyes. Talked to them. Kissed them. Called them Brother and Sister and Beautiful Girl. They are all around me, have always been. I just wasn't ready to notice. It is possible to be humble and arrogant at once. I think it's called courage. Time is running out. I feel I must do another line before going to work. (Cling, cling, cling.) Can't quite let go of the old ways. There are no punishments, only consequences in the Law. I'm certain of this though I don't know how. I'm not a sideshow ranter at a violent peep show! That's what I call poetry. But what does it mean? Who does it help? What veil does it lift? Falling by desire back to earth while spirit struggles to stay aloft. The two must meet half way to achieve harmony. The body serves the spirit, a guide in this densest forest. The spirit cares for the body so the whole may become...not gibberish. I just don't really understand yet. Letting off the steam. Too intense inside when I believe I'm all alone. Flip-flop. Back and forth again. How do I stand this crazy ride? Lot's of questions. That's good and ok. I'm heading home on the other side. The uncertainty will pass. Today will pass. I will make the best of this gift. I'm my own best teacher when I listen. I will calm my fears. I will let my True Will guide my actions. I will work hard so I may discover my True Nature and the powers of my Being. I will be alright.

Chapter 13

The Smile

I am in India, in retreat and for the first time in my life I *am* all right.

"Today we're going to go for a walk," Tim says. There is a holy place above Tushita and we are going to make a short pilgrimage there.

We sigh in relief at even the prospect of this welcome break, this diversion from silence and sitting. I blush with guilty pleasure. After five days of the routine of retreat, it sounds like an impossible indulgence, like a movie with popcorn and soda or a tray of chocolate éclairs.

This retreat has been nothing of the sort. It has been a full on offensive. For five days we have been marching headlong into unexplored regions of our minds. We have been challenged with new ideas and asked again and again to look ever deeper into who we really are. There is more pain here than I ever imagined, emotional as well as physical. I dredge it up like the muck and silt from a deep riverbed and some of it is older and darker than I'd like to own up to.

I've tried hard not to have any expectations about this retreat. I've tried to just take whatever comes up as being the thing to embrace. But the truth is I've brought a whole suitcase full of expectations. I imagined I would be bathing in spiritual ecstasy and realization by now, that there would be non-stop clairvoyance, revelations and the truth of myself unfolding in a heavenly shower of flower petals, perfume and nectar right before my eyes.

But instead I find that I'm sitting day after day on a hard, uncomfortable cushion on the floor of a cold, damp meditation hall. The cushion cuts into my veins and stops the flow of blood until my legs are cold and numb like two frozen lamb chops dangling useless from my hips. Sometimes, as I sit there with the others who shift and sneeze and cough, I can barely stay awake. The rain beats its fists against the windows in the last furious argument of the monsoon and sometimes it's hard not to be distracted and even afraid. Sometimes my body aches and moans so badly that I just want to get up and walk out in a huff of exasperation and self-righteousness. And then there are times that I just don't feel good enough to be here at all.

But then I remember the young woman who used to sit in front of me. If sitting is uncomfortable for me, it has been an unbearable torture for her. She has finally given up on the cushion and now sits on a chair to my right. She shifts and squirms in the silence and as she reaches around to massage the knotted muscles of her lower back we can all hear a tiny groan escape. Every minute for her is heat and pain. But still, she doesn't give up. Not ever. She endures the suffering because there is something worthwhile to be found here, with it and through it. After the sessions we take turns offering our condolences, our help, our sympathy and suggestions. But she just smiles and shrugs, "Oh well, I have back problems. I hoped it wouldn't bother me this much but what can I do?"

I have to jump up and spin a little pirouette at this. How amazing! Everyone here is making this huge effort to find out the truth about themselves and this tangled confusion of a world that we've all been thrown into. I am not alone. So I sit through my own little pain looking to the courageous woman to my right as a hero. I sit through the boredom and the wishing that I was somewhere else. I stop looking forward to the time when we will *really* start practicing. I let the dark memories of the past twenty years come up. I stop fighting and just do my best to try and let go.

Now it is after lunch and we have all gathered at the back door of the gompa. The sun is bright and warm and it soaks into our tired joints and muscles. Our bellies are full of vegetable soup and fresh bread and we all feel giddy at the prospect of leaving the retreat grounds for a little while. The hike, this mini-pilgrimage, is not required but no one has opted to stay behind.

We take the path that leads us off the grounds of Tushita, up into the mountain forest. After crossing the road to Dharamkot, the path narrows and we walk single file, stopping now and again to catch our breath at six thousand feet. The town of McLeod Ganj comes into view far below, a few haphazard buildings strewn across the top of a thin ridge. I can see Tsug Lhakang, the main temple of His Holiness the Dalai Lama, at the end. Jampa Deyki stops and faces it, touching her hands to her crown, throat and heart in a gesture of reverence. I want to do that too. I want to throw myself onto the ground, prostrating a hundred times like I've seen the Tibetans do. But instead, I succumb to propriety and pride and just fold my hands at my chest and offer a subtle bow.

We stop our march after twenty minutes and we pant and sweat at the entrance of a tiny path that leads into the thick part of the forest. Prayer flags stream from every tree, fluttering in the wind.

"It is only a little bit further," Tim whispers. "We are going to pass the huts of many meditators. Some of them are here on lifelong retreat." He turns and heads into the dark.

Lifelong retreat. I go chill and tingle as I try to comprehend what that means. This is the big view of Buddhism put into practice; the action and the sacrifice of the bodhisattva is to never waver from the goal of liberation for the sake of others. If that means spending a lifetime, or a dozen lifetimes, alone and in deep contemplation, then so be it. I look up the hill into the forest and wonder if could do that, if I could renounce the world of pleasure and gain all for the slim chance of finally waking up.

We file up the narrow path over hand cut, mossy stone steps. Through the trees I can see a half a dozen stone huts surrounded by neatly stacked granite walls. The roofs are made of old plywood and corrugated aluminum and I think they must turn into deafening percussion instruments in the heavy rains. Tiny chimney pipes puff out wisps of wood smoke and the smell of cooking rice. The yards are crisscrossed with prayer flags and red monk's robes draped over laundry lines. No one stirs inside any of them and the air is silent and still as we pass by.

We come into a tiny glen and on the opposite end are two *stupas*. Tim has told us that just by circling these holy monuments and making prayers around them, one is said to accumulate vast spiritual merit that will one day culminate in enlightenment.

But as I look at these two funny looking structures, squat bulbs on square foundations of grey stone with tall skyward reaching spires leafed in gold, I feel nothing. There is no spiritual fireworks show, no rainbow light emanating from them. If they do radiate some unseen power, I don't feel it.

Still, I approach them with reverence and respect. These two house the remains of two great meditation masters and teachers, realized beings who followed the Buddha's instructions to the letter and finally succeeded in their final goal of enlightenment.

I walk straight for the largest of the monuments and face it. I let my go of my pride and prostrate three times in front of it. Then I pull out my mala and following Tim's advice, start reciting the prayer I made up before we left.

May my spiritual practice flourish for the benefit of all beings, I begin.

It seems like not too much to ask and noble enough. But still I blush thinking, who am I to aspire to such things?

I round the stupa once, counting off a bead on my mala each time I say the prayer softly under my breath. I feel foolish at first and nervously glance around, worried that everyone is watching me and laughing to themselves at this green Buddhist. Still I keep going around, again and again, and I say the prayer until the noise of my fears is drowned out by the mantra.

I try not to expect too much, even though in the back of my mind I'm waiting for some sign carried by the wind in the trees or a voice or a vision. I'm looking for some confirmation that this is the path for me, some recognition that I've done this before in a place like this, in a life like this, like a deep calling to my soul. But that doesn't come at all and I finish my rounds and bow quickly before walking out of the gate, holding my disappointment in front of me, careful not to push it too far away. I've learned that much already.

I return to the group, which has already begun to gather in the small glen under the old, gnarled pines. I linger as they start to head out of the clearing and back down the mountain. I wait until they are out of sight before I follow, stopping every few feet, looking back, making sure I didn't miss something.

I trip over a mossy root hidden under brown rotting leaves and when I catch my balance and look up, there, outside the door of one of the stone huts, is a monk. He has a round, pleasant face and a plump belly. He is hanging his red monk's robes out to dry. He looks right at me and waves. His mouth is wide and I think, how is it possible for one face to hold such a smile? It is as big as an apple pie and his fat white teeth gleam in the sun that peeks through the trees above. It is the most genuine smile I have ever seen. He is happy and what's more he's happy to see me. *Me*, a total stranger. He waves and waves and though he doesn't say a word I know exactly what he means.

"Hello, dear friend! It's so nice to see you! Don't worry, we are the same, you and I and everyone else. All of us are OK!"

Doubt and disappointment fall away like leaves in November. I am not a failure. There is nothing to be ashamed of anymore. I am on the right path.

I wave back at my new friend then fold my hands and bow. He bows back and I turn to put one foot on the track in front of me. I start to skip and laugh. I skip and laugh all the way down the slippery steps until I catch up with the other pilgrims. I jump into their midst and plant my two feet hard into the ground and let out a hearty hoorah! And I feel, for the first time in a thousand years, like I'm finally a part of the human race.

Chapter 14

Clean

It is eight years before India. The beginning of the new millennium is only months away. Y2K. It is the end of the world. It is the beginning of the world and I am coming home to try sobriety for the first time.

The Colorado air is clean and cool but as I step off of the plane and take a deep breath it sears my lungs, raw from fifty thousand hits of crystal meth. I am nothing more than a skeleton now, a hundred and thirty pounds of bones and desperation. I am sunken eyes and death-ash skin. I am rotting teeth and bleeding gums. I am forgotten name and alone, shell shocked and trying to remember.

But now it all comes back to me. How could I forget? A thousand nights of higher and higher, with the drugs and the porn as my only purpose. Glass pipes and weed pipes, nitrous and bottles of beer set up in front of me like a surgeon's tool kit. A hit, a line, a drink, a drag and then a nod. *Don't nod off, not yet, only want to go to the edge of the other side*, I would say. And so, mind twisted and strange, I stared deep into those images on the little screen, digging deep to cut out the bloody tumors of my desire.

Still, I could never really own that desire, could never call it by its true name. I couldn't even see that it wasn't desire at all but the essence of the real me, the gay me, just trying to get out. So I took the drugs wildly, hoping they would help me to sound out that name with dry throat and tongue. I would snort whole grams of speed in one great inhale, stay awake and stuttering for days, make my way to the gay clubs and porno stores when I thought I had finally broken through. But even then I could only stand there on the shore of that sea of men and sex while the throbbing music and the desperate moans crashed over me like waves. Sometimes I would hold those men in the middle of the night, there in the dark little booths where I could get down on my knees and with open arms and mouth finally confess. But mostly I would just bite my lip till it bled and run for the door.

Three years I did this. Nine hundred blinding sunrises in a row. Then the bottom came up too fast and seeing the imminent future of me, shattered and broken there on the hard, concrete earth, I called home.

"Help, help, help!" I cried. But not for the help I needed. Just a quick fix and a place to run to and crash.

Now here I am in Colorado. Soon my family will embrace me, welcome me home and breathe an uncertain sigh of relief. But all the while they will shoot me cautious sidelong glances from the edge of uneasy memories and the anguish of all those years I spun further and further away will still be too raw to touch.

"He's come home," they will think. "But is he really ready?"

They will be right to worry but for now, with two old suitcases, my dog and a pocketful of the best intentions I think that the change has finally come. I tell myself that high up in the mountains, I will finally find my true self and resurrect him from his long burial. Good food, sleep and fresh air will be enough to make me grow strong again. The first snow will come and I will dance in it renewed. My addictions and obsessions will fall off like an old snake's skin.

I will work hard at my cousin's restaurant there in the mountains, make good on her and her husband's generosity. I think, too, that the small town life will do me good and I will forge new and wholesome friendships with the people and the land. I will become some newborn mountain man and the moose and the elk and the coyotes will all lean in close and whisper their names to me. So will the columbine, the aspen and the sage. The deep mountain lakes will be blue and cold and I will dip my fingers and toes in their clear, holy waters so I become clean and whole again.

But none of this will ever come true.

You see, fueled by a little success, my ego will grow bigger even than the Rocky Mountains that surround me and my bravado will echo through the land.

"I *used* to be a drug addict," I will say. "Now I am in control." Then I will take a big gulp of the beer in front of me and, without even knowing it, start the cycle anew.

All of the old, unresolved conflicts that I packed with me at the bottom of those two beat up suitcases will be standing right next to me. All through the long, dark nights of winter they will whisper in my ear bedtime stories of failure and shame. Then the bedtime stories will weave themselves into dreams of suicide and day after day I will wake curled up on the floor, head ringing from the booze and the wine, trying to forget.

Every morning I will look into the mirror, deep into my eyes and I will not like the person I see there at all. He will not be the dear old friend he should be but a disgusting man that no one could ever want or love. I'll slap him hard across the face and beat his chest until he chokes all of his bitter self-loathing down. And there it will grow like thick tangled roots in the cellar where he keeps all of his unwanted memories and scary truths. Down there in the dark he will hide all the men he ever slept with, all the longings he's ever had, all of the *terrible things he's ever done.*

"That's not me," I'll say. "That was just a phase. I'm normal now. I'm straight."

But I won't be able to swallow that bitter lie. I'll have to wash it down with gallons of gin and wine and beer. Everyday I'll need more and more until finally the day will come that I'll go into town for a drink but instead I'll have fifteen. I'll drink till I'm spinning and falling and screaming for more. I'll drink till I stagger back out into the blazing sun, into my car, laughing and drooling as I pull out the keys.

I'll make it ten miles down the long highway without a

scratch, squeezing one eye shut to stay in my lane, before spinning the wheel hard and tearing onto the dirt road. I'll turn up the radio and scream. Then, knowing I'm invincible, I'll punch the gas. Thirty miles an hour. Forty. Fifty. I'll skid and slide over the wash-boarded curves with my teeth rattling in my skull and as I come to the edges of the steep gullies and ravines, I'll just laugh like mad.

"Fuck it!" I'll shout. "Ain't death a hoot!"

It will all happen so fast that I won't have time to take it back. Suddenly, the world will explode in a blast of shattered glass and twisting metal. I'll go up and over, end over end. I'll come crashing down in a broken, steaming heap. I'll hang there upside down for a long while with the sun shining through the sparkling dust dancing in front of my eyes. It will be very quiet then, just a breeze in the creaking branches of the pines and the spinning whir of a mangled tire. And then, in the silence that follows, beautiful and almost perfect, I'll think *shit, I'm still alive*.

There will be no life flashing before my eyes. I will not be shaken out of my thick sleep. There will be no epiphany or realization of any kind. Instead I'll just crawl out of that wreck of my life, stalk around it like a hunter over his prey then kick it to make sure it's dead. Then I'll wipe the blood and the broken glass off my face and shoulders and without another thought or a word, I'll just walk away from my second attempt at suicide and order another drink...

As I head out of the airport on a fine fall day I don't know any of this. The taste of my last line is still chemical metallic on my tongue. I want to change. I really do. I just don't know that it's going to take work. And so with a little bit of hope and all those good intentions, I step into the clean air and smile like a naïve and trusting child.

.

Chapter 15

A Winding Road

"Hey, can you get me some of that shit," I whisper.

"Sure, man. How much ya need?"

And that is all it takes. Six months after the crash. Eighteen months without speed. Then a bump, the burn and another downward spiral.

This is the road of the long slow decline. You know it well. You who have watched helpless as son, daughter, sister, brother, husband, wife, friend stood uncertain at its crossroads before taking that single decisive step. Maybe you took that step yourself. Either way, you know that there is no getting off of this road until the traveler has reached its inevitable end. The road twists and winds and goes on into an unseen, distant horizon. Sometimes there are breakdowns. Sometimes there is hope. Sometimes the ones we love crash and die.

There may be rest stops along the way on this road, side trips into what looks like happiness or sanity. But these are only mirages that shimmer and dissolve when we reach out to grab them. They are not *real* life or *real* rest stops. In the end, the traveler must figure out why he got on the road in the first place before making that final choice to get off.

My road is a hundred thousand miles long and it will take me six more years to travel its full length before I finally find the courage to take the exit. In the mean time I will take many side trips of my own. A couple of good jobs. A trip abroad. A second shot at a relationship with a woman that was almost normal.

That one was good for a while and we were happy for some of it. She let me be wild and free, showed me how to wear flip-flops instead of my shoes that were always laced too tight. We howled together in an endless stretch of night and weeks would go by when we never saw the sun. We danced with the angels in downtown Denver, five twirling statues that watched silently over the graveyard of bars and last calls and they were *our* angels for a while, protecting us from harm.

But we were both hurt and wounded already and though we thought we were rubbing soothing balm into each other's wounds, it turned out to be just more salt and burning.

Four years we danced like mad. Cocaine every day. Drunk and high, high and drunk. Dark love mixed with the light. I was "straight" for much of it but finally the mask wore thin and eventually it fell away in tatters.

Then one night we got high and drunk enough for me to take on a lover while she watched and with that, the secret was out. So we took on another lover, then another. I thought it was exciting. I thought it was being the "real" me. But it was really just another mask.

Then the crack came and the pills too, until we finally crashed.

I hit the concrete median hard at a hundred miles an hour and the force of it broke the bones of my soul. I thought, "This is it. I need to get off of this road once and for all!" And so I picked up the mangled pieces of my body and mind, smoked one more rock and called home once again.

But the road doesn't end there. There are still long miles to go and tonight I drive a stretch of them in the snow and the wind and the ice back home. There, my mother greets me at the door and she bites her lip at the sight of me, swollen and red faced with a half dollar sized boil on my forehead, the whites of my eyes tea-stained yellow.

"I have a problem with drugs and alcohol," I told her on the phone. It took me over twenty years to say those words and it would still take me another two to believe them.

The Lord is gone now, his mania and madness finally too much to take and so it is good to be home, in a warm bed, with hot food and the care of family. I let my defenses down, let myself be cared for and I try to return that kindness with a real effort to change.

Today I walk through the front doors of the rehab center in Colorado Springs, into the face of the hard reality of who I have become. I am scared. I am frail and weak and shuddering while trying to hold my head high. The air smells like stale coffee and bleach. I squint into the bright fluorescent lights while the folding tables and chairs, set up in neat rows on the sparkling linoleum floor, tell me their tale of discipline and regulation. Then I see the Bible quotes posted on every wall. These scare me the most as I realize that no matter how scarred I am from belief, I will finally have to start believing in something in order to make this work.

I wait for the director while the receptionist watches me from the corner of his eye. I flip through the photocopied packet of rules. There will be no smoking, no visitors, no letters, no phone calls. There will be no tentative trial periods, no apologies, no excuses. There will be no failure allowed here at all, just my commitment to the program and my willingness to get sober.

I close the packet and stare out the window. The cold has come early this year. It is overcast December and I watch as the frozen air falls to the ground in a thin mist of fine powdered crystal. I am not ready for this. I want to give up right here and now, to run for the nearest bottle or line.

When I sit in the cramped office of the director, looking away from her unblinking gaze that sees right through my indecision and self-deception, I know that I'm not going to make it here. Even as I fill out the admission forms with the crooked black lines marked out for my life's story, I know that I'm not ready. Even as I write out my two-lined autobiography with a shaking, sweating hand, I know that this isn't going to work at all.

Started using alcohol and tobacco when I was twelve, I write. *Moved on to marijuana, LSD and psychedelics, then amphetamines, ecstasy, prescription drugs and crack cocaine.*

And even as I sit there stunned by the simple truth of it all, that I have not spent one day truly sober in twenty three years, I know that it is success, not failure, that is not going to be an option here. At least not yet anyway.

"My mom thinks I might be gay," I say.

I am having dinner with my second wife in Saigon Café. It is early spring 2006. I have been keeping a secret for over thirty-five years but now I try to blurt it out over a hot bowl of *pho thai*. I don't think about the words. I just say them. Then I hide behind the curtain of steam and vagueness that wafts between us, waiting for a hard slap across the face.

I have been more or less sober for four months now. This last stretch has gone on for almost sixty days. I am clearheaded for the first time in my life and in that clarity I have heard the faint voice of the self that has been patiently whispering to me all along.

In between the crack dreams and the drunk dreams that leave me sweating and shaking in the night, I have dreams of who I really am. In one of them, I am in a relationship with another man. We kiss as I watch us from above. He gets up and walks out into the street. Then the rain comes pouring down as I chase after him. He hides behind a tree on the side of the road and though I call out, he doesn't hear. Suddenly, I start moving incredibly fast and I float just above the surface of the earth. He calls my name as I pass him by, asking me to wait but I am so overjoyed that I can't stop. I start to fly, high into the air. I fly through the clouds and when I get into the open sky I leave the atmosphere almost instantly. The stars are brilliant and I set a course for the brightest one.

When I woke up from that dream I thought, "Today's the day I'm going to tell her."

But when I saw my wife coming up the stairs with a faint smile and eyes full of sleep, I just couldn't do it.

A few days later my mom told me she had a friend she wanted me to talk to. We were sitting out on the back porch. It was warm for February and neither of us wore a coat. Three young deer watched us from behind the tall brown grass on the hill behind the house. I hid my head in my hands from them, ashamed of sneaking out the day before on a secret relapse. She put her hand on my shoulder, told me her friend was alcoholic for years before he finally found the courage to tell his wife he was gay.

I looked up at her amazed. There she was smiling at me, her eyes filled with real tenderness and I thought for sure that I knew what they said.

"I know and I am so sorry."

My *mom* thinks I *might* be gay.

It is not the noble and courageous statement of liberation that I had rehearsed in my mind for the past four months. I wanted to sit down with my wife, hold her hands gently in mine and tell her:

"Sweetheart, I'm gay. I'm so sorry that I didn't tell you sooner but I was so afraid and I didn't want to hurt you. I didn't want to hurt myself…"

Instead I fumble and waffle and flip-flop. My shoulders slump and I wince with eyes squeezed shut.

"*Really?*" she says. "Well what do *you* think?"

"Well, I…I don't know. Sometimes I think so but…" Then I retreat again.

I reach out to take a sip of lukewarm jasmine tea hoping to fill the chasm of disappointment that is opening up in my chest. Then she just goes back to her soup while I go slinking back into the closet.

We won't speak about this again for another six months. But still, I have proven that I am almost ready. The end of the road is in sight.

One more relapse should do it.

Chapter 16

An Offering of Light

"Do not be heavy," Soen Roshi says. *"Be light, light, light—full of light!"*
~ Peter Matthiessen

Today is my last day in Tushita. It is mid October now but it is still warm in India. I breathe in the sunlight and the pine and the silence, take all these things in like nourishing food and water.

I go to the gompa now to pick up the bronze bell one last time. I ring it loud and clear on the steps outside and the heads and bodies of lounging retreaters pop up from the lawn and garden like prairie dogs greeting the rising sun.

"Time is so precious," I think as I make the rounds. "It is so easy to let it slip by unnoticed."

I walk up the stone steps slowly, trying hard to be mindful, resolving to be present as I feel each step under my feet. I breathe slowly too and swing the mallet with all my attention focused on this moment.

"This is the last time I am going to ring this bell here, in this time and place," I think.

I am grasping too hard. In my heart, I want this moment to last, to never be forgotten. But this is not the lesson of mindfulness and so it slips away.

It is midday now and forty-eight western seekers lay out on thin straw mats on the rooftop of the meditation hall. We are tired and sore from ten days of sitting cross-legged and our minds are tangled too with all the new information from the long teachings.

"Where is the 'you' who was five years old?" Jampa Deyki had asked just this morning.

We were restless, agitated, on the verge of outright revolt as our teacher introduced us to the most difficult topic in Buddhist philosophy: Emptiness. She was calling into question the very ground on which we all placed our view of reality, of how we saw ourselves and all of the people and things in our lives.

"Let's take a moment to look for that solid, real, independently existing 'I' that we believe has always been there," she said. "This is the 'I' that comes to center stage every time you want something or feel threatened or are faced with something you absolutely don't want. Where is it? What does it look like? Is it in your body, your fingers, your toes, your stomach? Is it in your brain or is it somewhere outside of you? Remember, it could be very small so be sure to look everywhere."

And so, along with all the others, I sat and searched until my head started to ache. But as hard as I tried, I couldn't find that elusive "I" anywhere. Every time I thought I had it, it just slipped away like a fine mist through my fingers. It wasn't my body whose very cells were in constant flux. It wasn't anywhere to be found in my shapeless, colorless, sizeless mind either. Nor was it my beliefs, my habits, my desires, my loves, my hates.

Suddenly, I realized that there was never any promise that something solid or real existed in the first place. I was not the person I was the day before. And all I ever tried to hold onto or even just perceive was different too. The trees outside the gompa were different. The clouds were different. The people on retreat with me were different. Tim was different. Venerable Jampa Deyki was different. My mind had changed and so had all those people and things.

Where was the "me" of five years old? I couldn't even tell where the 'me' from two years ago was. Two years ago that "me" was still pale and shivering in the closet, clutching desperately at a bottle of booze and a baggie of cocaine. That 'me' couldn't even imagine India or the Buddha or limitless love and compassion.

Then, for just a fleeting moment, I saw that nothing was fixed, permanent or real in the sense that I had always so desperately wanted to believe.

And sometimes, I thought, that can be a very, very good thing.

But now, all of us are solid again. We are deep in our solid thoughts. We are wondering who we are. We are not sure if we exist. Richard, our Russian yoga instructor, scans our tired faces then wrinkles his nose, puzzled.

"What was the topic this morning?" he asks.

"Emptiness," a student croaks in despair.

"Ah emptiness," he laughs. Then he reads all our minds and smiles.

"Don't worry!" he shouts. "You exist!"

And so he goes easy on us on our last day. There will be no twisting our bodies into complicated knots or touching our heels to our ears. Instead he has us gently breathe and stretch until we are loose and relaxed in the warm Indian sun. Then we simply sit.

"Now I want you to bring up your right leg over the left," he says.

His voice is so calm and I think I would do anything he asked.

"Now hold your right knee with your arms and let your head hang down, looking towards your belly. Let yourself completely go and focus all your attention there. Through meditation and looking deeply within, many things will come up. Many short-comings and fears will arise."

As I follow the sound of Richard's voice I find myself relaxing more and more. I let my attention rest there in my belly and allow all the feelings of unworthiness and disappointment with myself to well up. I don't try to push them back down or deny them. They are simply there and I can resist or embrace them as I like. It is my choice.

With my face hidden there in my arms, I begin to realize that it's ok to feel vulnerable and afraid. It's ok that I spent years hiding the truth about myself. It's ok that I was lonely and angry and a little bit crazy. It's ok that I hurt myself and even the ones I love. It's ok that I made so many mistakes. Right here, right now all can be acknowledged, all can be forgiven.

As I embrace all of these shortcomings I begin to feel myself let go. The merciless inner critic who used to slash me down to the bone is silenced and for the first time in years, maybe even for the first time in my whole life, I feel real compassion for myself. Finally, I see the reality of my own suffering and I am not so afraid of it anymore.

I lift up my head and the sun is still shining warm on my shoulders. I look around and see that there are many sets of glistening eyes looking right back at me. It is a good sight, not a sad one. I know now that all of these people have seen something good and fertile and rich within themselves and that they too have decided to keep it and till it into the deep soil of their lives. I take a slow, deep breath, the kind that hurts your lungs after a long cry; then I let it go.

It is a still and quiet night as we all gather out on the lawn; even the monkeys are silent, asleep in the branches of the trees. This is our last night together. We have done it! We have sat together in silence, supported one another in our deep looking. And even though we haven't spoken in ten days, it seems that we know each other better now than lifelong friends.

We sit on the dew-wet grass and before us is the stupa. We have made our final offering of light there, three candles each that we set gently on its little steps that go up, up to the pinnacle of enlightenment. We offered these as lights in the darkness of ignorance for ourselves, for our loved ones, for those we don't even know.

Now the golden light of our offering illuminates our faces as we chant, softly at first, *Om Mani Padme Hum*. Our voices grow stronger, soaring in the night and for just a little while they become one voice. Then we taper off into a comfortable silence here under the stars.

Illuminated in body and mind we dedicate the merit of what we have done together on this short retreat. One brave voice begins and soon we are writing a long, spontaneous love poem together. It is a poem dedicated to all suffering sentient beings and we recite it in our own voices, in our native tongues: Hebrew, German, Dutch, French and English. And even if we don't always understand all of the words, the meaning is as powerful as a building storm.

The hairs on my neck stand on end and I shiver. I have never felt such sincerity, such kindness, such pure and good belief in action. After all the talk of enlightenment and liberating countless beings from the suffering of beginningless lives, it all comes down, right here and now, to the real love and compassion that ordinary human beings can have for one another. It doesn't matter if we are Buddhist or Christian or Muslim or Jewish or even no religion at all. We can all make prayers together and wish the best for everyone.

I sit and wait, half-expecting some kind of mystical welcome mat to be laid out just for me. I wait for my own revelatory words to shine on my tongue like starlight but instead, all I find is all the ordinary stuff that's still here inside me. I look around at the golden faces and see that lots of other people are just as fragile and ordinary as I am, all of them searching for some sense in a crazy world. And now, as the hard shell that has secreted itself around my heart finally cracks open, I find that I am deeply in love with all the world.

Now I offer up my own prayer of dedication from this big, new heart. My voice shakes and trembles at first. But then I feel the support of everyone around me and with growing confidence and certainty I offer all of my effort, hard work and honesty of the past year. I offer every apology I've made to the family and friends who I've hurt through my years of addiction. I offer my understanding and appreciation of how far I've come. I offer all of my weakness, my shortcomings and my frailties too, all of the things that I hope will one day make me wise.

When it is all over I wait for the feelings of fulfillment and completion to wash over me. But the wave never comes. Instead, I am filled with an ordinary kind of emptiness. It is a sad longing that I do not understand. This should be it, I think. The final realization, the rush of enlightenment, the ultimate fix of liberation.

We gather our blankets and mats and head off into the dark to our rooms. I wrap myself tight in my scratchy wool blanket and fall into a fitful sleep full of strange dreams. In the last one, I am in the deep end of a dark pool. I am flailing my arms, trying hard to keep my head above the surface.

"Oh no," I scream as I sink, taking in great gulps of the cold water. "The retreat is almost over and nothing has changed at all!"

I wake, gripping my blanket. One of my roommates groans and turns over in his sleep and I can just make out the rise and fall of his chest there in the half moon light.

Tomorrow the silence will be over. We will pack our things and head back down to the noise and bustle of McLeod Ganj. There we will meet for a celebratory meal at Nick's Italian Kitchen and order ravioli and lasagna made by Indian and Tibetan cooks. We will pull long tables together on the open patio overlooking the valley below. We will feast and laugh and speak to one another for the first time. We will learn each other's names, where we went to school, our job titles, our politics, our hobbies, our histories. I will laugh with the others for a while but then I will grow quiet, sipping on a dusty old bottle of Sprite while I shy away from the cameras and the conversations. I will wonder if I have learned anything at all. Then I will look again at the faces of my new friends, knowing that we will soon go our own ways. And as I sit there wishing that the silence had never ended at all I will think: something has to change.

Chapter 17

Coming Out

You can explore the universe looking for somebody who is more deserving of your love and affection than you are yourself, and you will not find that person anywhere.
~ The Buddha

The crack pipe shakes in my hand as I take short, nervous drags off my cigarette. This is relapse, take one hundred. I can only remember bits and pieces of this long and hopeless night but they tell the story clear enough. There was that first drink at the bar, then shots of liquor and a wild, cackling scream: *Where's the cocaine!!!* There are just flashes of images after that, staggering around the streets of the city but nothing else until I come to at a crack party at an old friend's apartment. I remember locking myself in the bathroom with one of my junkie friends, begging him to let me suck him off after I took a hit. Then I blacked out again.

But now I am wide-awake and aware of every sound, taste and smell. The air is still and stale, kept close by thick drapes that block out light and prying eyes. The house is empty except for a friend passed out in a five-day cocaine stupor on the thrift store couch in the living room. My wife sits behind me, bored and high, flipping through a tattered tabloid magazine. I try to ignore her as I keep my eyes glued to the random mix of porn streaming across the computer screen in front of me. I click back and forth between gay scenes and straight scenes like I'm shopping for the deal of the century.

"Ya know," she says finally. "Your obsession with porn is unnatural."

I shove another hit into the pipe, light the rock until I hear that familiar hiss and sizzle. I suck in the smoke violently, recklessly, before exhaling a crystalline cloud of chemical courage.

"Babe, I think I might be gay." I spit it out with the hit like a hot coal.

For months the pressure has been building. All I have thought about is how to tell her. But after that night in Saigon Café, I could never find the right moment again, could never find the right words, could never find the courage. So our lives deteriorated into one long blur of suicide drinking matches, screaming, clawing and fighting while I set up roadblocks and sabotaged myself every step of the way.

Do not pass go 'til coming out.

"What are you talking about?" she says. She sets the magazine down and her eyes burn through me as she takes a long drag of her cigarette.

I get up and point frantically at the computer.

"You see that?" I say. "Don't you get it?" It's so obvious to me and I become feverish, ranting and raving as I tap the face of the pretty girl having sex on the glass screen with a manic finger.

"I'm not interested in *her*, Babe. I want to *be* her!"

The words hang uncomfortably in the space between us and for a long while there is nothing but silence.

Then she laughs.

"You're serious aren't you?" she says.

"Yes," I say.

"Oh my god, you're serious."

She pushes a thin breath through tightly pursed lips and I think she's going to start hyperventilating. Her shoulders slump forward and when I see her there looking defeated and broken, all I want to do is take it all back.

"Oh my god," she says again as the future flashes before her. "What the fuck am I supposed to do now?"

There is nothing to say so I just sit there, holding a crack pipe and a cigarette, thinking I am the biggest piece of shit on the planet.

She starts to laugh again and the hairs on my neck stand on end. This time it's an eerie laugh, a crazy laugh, a laugh laced with denial. She shakes herself off and reaches for her own pipe, lights the end and takes another hit.

"Maybe we can just be best friends," she says. "Maybe…"

But there is no maybe. The door to the closet is open now, wider than ever. And though I still don't want to walk through it, there is no shutting it now. No taking back what I've said. Now it's only a matter of time.

Two days later and I am drunk on the second story porch of our cottage house apartment. I think: coming out is a battle and drinking is a shield; there are enemies everywhere, real and imagined. Mostly imagined. What are my friends going to think? What is my Dad going to think? What is my brother going to think? I am thirty-six years old. I should have figured this out by now.

I do the shuffle one last time before inching into that icy-cold lake called freedom a little more, a little more. Better just to jump in headlong, take the shock and get it over with. But the water looks so cold!

So instead I am drunk and pretending to be fearless. But really I am scared out of my mind.

My good friend has come down from Denver to be with me and I am raging around to a heavy metal song called simply, *Faggot*. "I'm just a faggot!" goes the chorus and the final refrain. An angry chant. Self-loathing and self-mockery. Still not able to embrace myself. Still not wholly convinced.

I break down and collapse on the floor.

"It just hurt so much to tell her." I start to sob, long and slow.

Ben, my best friend for all these long years of chaos, has been watching me rant and rave the whole time. Has he been waiting for honesty and authenticity? Well, here it is. Finally. So he says come here and I let my face rest on his shoulder and soak his shirt with real tears, warm and salty. My eyes are swimming in them and my heart feels like a broken piece of pottery all over the floor. What am I going to do?

Ben looks at me. He is drunk too but more coherent. He came out years ago and has had time to heal. He's made peace with himself. He knows.

"That feeling you're feeling right now?" he says. "That's why we march."

I look up at him, see he is smiling from the other side and for a moment, I begin to understand.

I've been out of the closet for only a month when I find myself pinned down in the back seat of the car. We have just come from the funeral of a friend who died from crack cocaine. Her sister and her son, two people I once called friends, are beating me half to death. We are drunk and angry and I have just said something stupid.

"She had it coming to her," I heard myself slurring under my breath.

Now I take what's been coming to me for years and I will never again feel this afraid, this alone, this powerless. Flailing fists smash my face, sending electric shocks of violence to my brain. Fingernails tear at my eyes and I think: "She's going to scratch my eyes out. She wants me to go blind."

"Faggot, faggot, you fucking faggot!" they scream. *Or are they saying, "Fly caged bird, fly"?*

I think I will go deaf from the screams that are filled with hate and loud enough to shatter a stone heart. But my heart is not stone; it is flesh and muscle beating two hundred times a minute as I start fighting for my life…

Bruised, sore and still bleeding, I wake up with my left eye swollen shut. I look in the mirror and realize I can't hide the truth any more. I pick up my phone, scroll through until I find my brother's number. I hesitate. I'm so scared. I hit "Send" anyway and the phone begins to ring.

"Hello?"

"Steve?"

"What? What's the matter?"

There is a pause, a space, then a leap into the unknown.

"Steve, I need to tell you something."

Chapter 18

Rebirth

Time passes unhindered. When we make mistakes, we cannot turn back and try again. All we can do is use the present well.
H.H. The XIV Dalai Lama

Up, up, up I climb. Up into Rocky Mountain foothills; up into the heart of my fears and limitations. The whoosh of the highway is now far in the distance as the still air becomes thin and clear. Cool rivers of sweat pour from my temples running fast down my neck and back.

Today, six months before heading off to India, I am alive!

I walk a furious pace, over the craggy landscape, through awakening sage and scrub oak, bound and determined to conquer these seven miles that have turned me back a dozen times. But five months without cigarettes or liquor now and my lungs feel like new. I breathe in deep at the two-mile mark, the start of the long loop trail, and pause.

I will not turn back this time. I will not give up. I have come too far, too fast.

Five months old now. A new born and delighted at the rush of senses only just discovered. I think back, remembering that first day, the day of my rebirth.

I can see myself coming home from the short vacation I took just after coming out. I thought I should celebrate. But now, standing outside the airport waiting for my ride, I look long and hard at the crumpled pack of Camels in my hand. My eyes follow down, down as they fall away into the trash and I dive in after them in my mind, trembling at the thought of walking the path ahead without my dear old crutch.

But then a shout from my cousin's husband in the pick up

lane and I hop into the truck.

"Whoa, you smell like booze!" he says.

"One last bender," I say. One last desperate grasp at the old way. One last bout with the hammer over my head. But then I imagined my new life out of the closet, stained by the same old tired songs of abuse and shuddered.

I remember the vow. *Never again.* I do not speak it out loud. I keep it close and secret, afraid that the power of it will evaporate like a wisp of cloud in the wind. And so we drive home where I will live with my cousin and my aunt and the hope of one last chance.

Four days later without a drink or a cigarette and the cravings come in powerful waves that threaten to bowl me over.

"Just one drag, just one drink and it will all go away," say the voices of old demons still squatting in a back room in my mind.

"Stay quit, stay quit, stay quit," says another voice, a voice that I am just learning to trust, a voice that I'm beginning to recognize as my own.

I chant the mantra to myself when the bargaining and the drafting of new promises begin and the demons withdraw.

Stay quit, stay quit, stay quit.

I am in the doctor's office cold and half naked as the skin of my thighs sticks to black vinyl. My heart beats a furious rat-tat-tat as the nurse takes blood pressure and pulse. Did he just whistle faintly through his teeth? Is he amazed that I am still alive?

I am. In fact, I am certain that I am dying. Two weeks sober and in the clarity memories flood back from two decades of abuse. No one could have come out of that unscathed. So I toss and turn for long nights, searching for lumps and tumors in my throat. I am certain that the numbness in my fingertips, the aches in my chest, the bulging veins I never noticed before, the muscle spasms near my left shoulder blade and above my right eye are all signs of an imminent end.

"Three-twenty-four," a bright voice says. The doctor has appeared out of nowhere to read the mysterious number from his laptop chart.

"What?" I snap out of morbid fantasies of my funeral that I watch, disembodied from above.

"Cholesterol. Your blood work came back. Your cholesterol. It's three-twenty-four."

I feel faint, woozy as I feel my blood pumping hard and fast through narrowing veins. It sounds bad.

"Is that bad?" I ask.

"It will be if you don't do something about it."

He is stern but kind and soon I find myself pouring my heart out to him. I tell him my story in fifty words or less. I am gay. I have just come out. I am two weeks sober. I am living with family and I'm trying to stay clean on my own.

He doesn't blink or roll his eyes. He doesn't shift uncomfortably in his swivel seat. He is used to this sort of honesty, like a priest taking confession. He listens with all his attention then after the calm of gathering thoughts he gives me a prescription. He tells me about Twelve Steps. He tells me about medication. He tells me about vitamins and eating better and exercise. He tells me I can do it, but not alone. I take it all in, open now to advice and wisdom that only a few months ago I would have shooed away like a moth flapping by my ear. But now I have promised myself I will try anything.

So I do. In a week I get up the courage to go to an AA meeting. There is warmth there, and love and support but there is something missing, like there is something else calling to me from just around the corner. I read through the Blue Book. I tear out big fat strips of fearless moral inventory, making amends and taking ownership. I toss them all into a crock-pot and cook up my own nourishing stew of recovery.

Body. Mind. Soul. Spirit. These I have neglected and now they call out to me in unison. They call out for attention and healing.

First I declare war on the enemies of my body. They have been hiding in the tree line, camouflaged and disguised as *license*, *reward* and *freedom*. But now I flush them out like spies and traitors, hunting down and driving out all their agents and co-conspirators. Sugar, caffeine, fast food, French fries, bacon, cheese, butter and grease, I rout them all out, send them retreating to the hills. I don't give in to their cries for mercy. Instead, I eat good food, fresh food, green food from the good earth. I listen to my body and let it tell me what it needs. It knows, it has always known.

Every morning, I reach down to touch my toes. At first, the pain is unbearable, muscles flabby and unused for years. But I take it slow. Stretch, do not strain. Sit-ups then push ups. An easy work out. Ten minutes a day. I hate it. I love it. I do it no matter what.

In two weeks my blood is tested again. Just like that I am back to normal. No drugs, no treatment, no pharmaceutical courtship.

It's a tiny victory, proof that I can change.

I am still scared. I am on new ground that shifts and sometimes even crumbles under my feet. I do not even know how to stand, how to walk, how to run. But I put one foot out anyway, hoping it will touch solid earth.

I read old journals, my diaries of confusion and despair, filled with drunken ramblings and cheap shots at a self that cries out for love. The repression so obvious now, a life filled with so much turmoil and fear. But here and there, clues and glimmers of hope. *I want to explore Tibetan Buddhism*, I wrote in big, sloppy letters across the top of one page. I remember it now, The Calling, clear and ringing out of the fog of fifteen beers, cocaine and a cloud of smoke. I just wasn't ready to hear it.

But I answer the call now. I stride into the little bookshop that I have passed a hundred times, with purpose and certainty. I march down the aisle to the three shelves marked Buddhism, breathe in the aroma of old musty books stacked haphazardly on floor and shelves. I let my fingers caress their spines, close my eyes and read the titles like Braille, absorbing their essence through my skin.

I find the one. My breath quickens. *The Tibetan Book of Living and Dying*. It jumps into my hands from the shelf up above. I flip to a random page and read. Yes, this is the one.

I cradle it in loving arms all the way home, down the stairs and into my room. I am giddy as I read. The words resonate in my mind like a melody forgotten or a poem I once knew by heart. With each turn of the page, each soaring Ah-ha, certainty grows. The ideas and concepts seem so familiar. I can't explain why or claim to understand it at all, but they ring in a high, clear note that shatters years of doubt.

The book is filled with stories of Tibet and they take me to the high places there. Tears run down my cheeks as I read the words of the Rinpoches, Buddhas in the flesh, who teach compassion with every breath. Impermanence, suffering, devotion, discipline, concentration, meditation, liberation. This is what Buddhism is all about and it is so much more than I ever imagined. I close the cover and all I want is more, more, more.

So I read. I read like I've never read before. In five years I've choked down two airport horror novels. Now I read two books a week. Life after death, quantum physics, Vedanta. I read the life stories of the Buddha and the Dalai Lama. I read the story of a western Zen student who spent six months in a monastery in Japan and was changed forever. I read Robert Thurman, Shunryu Suzuki, Milarepa, Sommerset Maugham, Jack Kornfield, Alexandria David-Neel, Peter Mattheissen, Santideva, Thomas Merton, Walpola Rahula, Herman Hesse and the Dalai Lama.

I read anything that stirs my curiosity but always I come back to Tibetan Buddhism, like a compass needle pointing north or a stream rushing to meet the big river that leads to the sea.

I fly high on the wings of the spirit, spin and glide free in the heavens. But when I look down and see the ground far below, I become afraid again. What if I fall? My heart is still heavy, weighed down by the unresolved past that threatens to send me crashing helplessly to the hard earth.

I have so many wounds. Most of them self-inflicted. I cannot heal them all by myself. So I get help. I find a healer, someone who will listen. It is slow and unpleasant and difficult work, digging through the layers of the past. But we work through it together, this kind elder and I. Slowly and patiently, she guides me to my own wisdom, teaches me how to love myself again.

I stand in front of the mirror day after day following her simple instructions.

"I love you," I say to myself.

At first I feel foolish. I don't believe it. So I look deep into my eyes and say it again. Then again. Then again. Then again. *I love you, I love you, I love you!* Weeks go by then months. Soon it doesn't matter how silly this is or who's ears might be pressed to the door. I look into that mirror and deep into those eyes every morning, every night. *I love you, I love you, I love you!*

Then slowly, very slowly, I start to believe it.

Soon, I find myself sprinkling little acts of kindness towards myself throughout the day. A kind word or a smile as I pass my reflection in a window. A gentle caress when I feel overwhelmed. A deep breath. A massaging of tired shoulders. A wish for happiness for myself and everyone I know. And then, without even noticing that it's happening, I begin to realize that I am my own best friend.

But this is only the beginning. There is still one last dragon to slay, snarling and gnashing its teeth right there on the path in front of me. I know I can't go any further unless I face it. So finally, standing on solid ground and trembling only a little, I take the next step.

We round the lake at Memorial Park for the third time and the storm clouds over Pikes Peak are held at bay by the power of our conversation. We have been talking deeply for almost an hour, this after barely speaking for a year. Three hundred and sixty five days of carefully orchestrated avoidance. Bristling at the sight of one another. Walking on eggshells.

But now the walls are down. The truth has been freed from its cage and there is nothing left of me that can be hurt.

"Mom, I'm gay." There. I have said it. It is done.

Droplets of rain begin to fall, welcome cool in the hundred degree heat of July summer.

"Ya know," she says. "I've never told anyone this."

I smile down at her, my mother, who used to loom before me and terrify me.

"When you were born, the hospital was out of blue blankets. So ya know what they did? They brought you to me wrapped in a pink one. I should have known then."

I exhale a little laugh through my nose and smile wider.

"Signs and portents," I say. "Signs and portents."

I wake up grateful. I am here; I am alive. It's been five months since my last drink and I am out of the closet and free.

I face the batik wall hanging of the Buddha I have placed above a simple altar of candles, incense, a single flower. I fold my hands. I bring them to my crown, my throat, my heart. I drop to my knees then stretch out my body accordion like on the floor until my forehead touches the ground. I reach out my arms as far as I can, lift up the fingertips in one last gesture of reverence. Then I get back up and do it again.

I am nervous. This feels awkward and strange. I wonder if anyone is awake and can hear my breathing getting faster and faster as I prostrate over and over again. What would they think if they could see me? I do a hundred and eight repetitions and when I am finished I am panting and pouring sweat.

Then I stack the pillows from my bed one on top of the other, a makeshift cushion. I recite the words of the Refuge Prayer even though I only suspect what they mean.

I take refuge until I am enlightened in the Buddha, the Dharma and the Sangha.

By practicing generosity and the other far reaching attitudes: ethics, patience, joyous effort, meditative concentration and wisdom,

May I attain Buddhahood for the benefit of all beings.

Then I sit, back straight, not proud but with great dignity. I clasp my hands in my lap, thumbs pointing upward and lightly touching. My eyes are full of sleep and I yawn.

I try to remember the instructions again, so simple yet so elusive. Don't force anything. Don't intend anything. Sit and watch the breath. Then the thoughts rise like high, cresting waves in a storm. But I keep trying to come back to the breath. Breathe in...one. Breathe out...one. Breathe in...thoughts, thoughts, thoughts. But it's ok. I sit for twenty minutes, foot asleep. I sit until I can't sit any more.

When I get up I write in my journal. I write about how happy I am. I write about how difficult it still is, how I will never be able to say with certainty that I will never fall back. I write myself love notes, and words of encouragement. I forgive myself. I am gentle with myself.

Then I go to the mountain. Today, I will finish the trail. I haven't felt this good in years. I will make my way to the high point. Eight thousand feet. It will be cold and the wind will bite even at the end of winter. But I will still feel warm. I will look around, seeing that I am alone in the great expanse. Alone but not lonely. The mountain will rest in front of me testifying to its own weight and presence.

Then I will skip down the narrow path shouting out loud, "I am going to make it!" Almost seven miles when only days ago a flight of stairs left me winded. When I get to the trailhead I will leap up, click my heels and cheer. I will look back up the mountain and then, smiling, heart soaring and breathing heavy, I will know that it's the little victories that are the best.

I have decided. I am going to India! There is nowhere else that I wish to go, no other goal that would be more worthwhile. I am afraid, afraid that it is too big a task, afraid that I might fail or falter or fall. But I don't care. I refuse to let my fear rule my life for one more minute.

Now is the time to study and prepare. All the money and energy that I used to spend on getting high are now available to me. All the restless energy of addiction can now be funneled in a new direction: Forward!

I go to work at the restaurant everyday with this burning purpose and resolve. The shiny bottles of booze are no longer a temptation, just baubles and widgets. My coworkers and my boss cheer me on. They like the new me and want him to stick around.

Goals and the possibility that I might actually attain them keep me awake at night. I lie there with eyes wide open imagining all the challenges that await me. Malaria, heat, sickness, culture shock, language and giant insects fill my mind with a delightful terror.

"Guess what?"

"What?" say the guests at the bar.

"I'm going to India…for two months!"

Blank stares and confusion. I am getting used to these. I try to answer the question "Why?"

To live for two months by my wits and with no more than I can carry on my back. Isn't that reason enough?

But there's more. There is the call of pilgrimage. Sarnath and Bodhgaya, Lumbini and Kushinigar, the four holy places of Buddhism call out to me. But of these I do not speak, afraid that I will break the spell.

I hang a calendar above my desk and begin to tick off the days. Six months to go. I have all the time in the world but still, there is not enough. There is so much to plan, so many thousands of little things to get done. It becomes my new obsession, my great problem and I wear it down like a boulder blocking my path with a piece of silk. I read, I study, I watch, I listen. I talk to those who have gone before me and make new friends. *Can I actually do this?* I laugh. Yes, I can!

Where is the man who used to rage and cry and beg for death? He is gone but not forgotten.

Rejoice in this life right now! Every moment is a gift, every breath an opportunity to be aware and to wake up. Time is slipping away!

Only a year ago a shameless, hopeless drug addict. Only a year ago drunk and blacked out. But now I look at how far I've come. If I pat myself on the back everyday then so be it. I know my weakness. I know that I could fall back into that life at any time.

So I congratulate myself to remind myself how far I have to fall, to remind myself how much I have to lose and to remind myself how important it is to love and respect myself.

I needed the discipline of sobriety, of meditation, of compassion to bring me here. But most of all I needed the discipline of self worth. Everyday I look at myself in the mirror with love and I know I am worth the effort.

Now all has been forgiven, all sins admitted and confessed. This is purification, nothing left to regret. The past has happened but now it is over and done. All this time I thought I had an eternity to live. But I don't. None of us do. So I promise myself I won't waste anymore time. It's time to live today. It's time to go on pilgrimage...

Chapter 19

Refuge

Be islands unto yourselves, refuges unto yourselves, seeking no external refuges, with the Dharma as your island, the Dharma as your refuge.

~ The Buddha

It is before Tushita, a few days before retreat, and I am going to see the Dalai Lama. I am going to become a Buddhist. I just don't know this yet.

The bus that will take me there from Delhi is an hour late. Plenty of time to stare, dumfounded and open-mouthed, into the face of India as I wait by the side of the road. I am clutching a sweaty bus ticket while she stares back at me, unblinking and unashamed, with a hundred thousand expressions to fit a hundred thousand moods. She is the young leper girl without a nose in bright blue sari begging for rupees while she dances and twirls to *tabla* beats. She is the prostitute leading the young man into the abandoned, graffiti covered shack across the street. She is the cars, auto-rickshaws and motorcycles screaming endlessly by. She is the three-legged dog covered in mange darting through the traffic.

This is not the face of India that I had expected or imagined. She is not draped in colorful silk or anointed with perfume. She is not sitting in the lotus posture chanting *Om*. There are no serenading sitars, no wafting clouds of curry and incense billowing around her and it is hard not to judge.

I watch as the shadows on her face lengthen and darken in the gathering dusk until the bus finally arrives. A young bus *wallah* leans out the door, collects the gaggle of westerners heading to Dharamsala and points us urgently to our seats. They call this the "Deluxe Bus" but as I look around I have to wonder at the name. Maybe they mean the air-conditioning system, a series of ancient fans hanging from the ceiling, all caked with dust, their frayed electric wires running off to no-where. Or maybe it's the thin membrane of rotting yellow foam on the hard plastic seats that barely softens the blows to my tailbone as we lurch into the night.

I do not sleep as we barrel down the mad Indian highway all through the night. Instead, I gaze out at the wild, weaving traffic and strain to pick out the melody in the crazy tune of a billion honking horns. I endure parched mouth and swollen tongue as I imagine the five days of teachings to come. What will he be like, His Holiness, this simple monk, this Buddha in the flesh? Will I be blinded by the sight of him or will my heart just explode?

At five a.m. my head stops rattling against the window. Flat tire. I rejoice at the chance to close my eyes and dream, even if it means being stranded here in the middle of nowhere. But the driver and his helpers have done this a thousand times before on this broken old bus, on this deserted road. They change tire, wheel, axle, engine and all like a pit stop crew and too soon we are off again, up, up into the foothills of the Himalayas.

The sun is rising now and I stare out the window through bloodshot eyes. Green hills roll up into the morning mist. Concrete block homes plastered with billboard ads for Epson, Cannon, Castrol, Kodak and Coca-Cola give way to thatched roofed houses with buffalo tethered in front yard gardens.

The bus crawls up the mountain now, a gasping old mare, her tired heart straining, sputtering and groaning through switch-backs and hairpin turns. We cross gushing streams swollen from monsoon rains and the brakes hiss and steam in the freezing water. I think we are not going to make it, that we are going to tumble back down the mountain to a bloody and mangled end.

But finally, seventeen hours after leaving Delhi, we arrive at the bus stand, a meeting of four roads at the top of McLeod Ganj, the hillside station that is now a bustling enclave of Tibetan refugees. It is eleven in the morning as I step off the bus into this "India Light". I had heard someone call it that but to me there is nothing light about it at all. To me everything here is intense and strange.

It is the noise that fills me with joy and dread! The constant growl and buzzing of diesel engines and motorbikes. The haggling in the marketplace over the price of kale, fresh apples and rice. The clop-clop of cow hooves. And always, always the honking of horns. So many languages, so many bodies, so many faces! It is the air too, filled with a wafting wall of cooking smoke and sweat, dung and sewer, ripe fruit and rotting wood. I take in a deep breath of it and I find that I am not offended. Instead, I stand firmly in the midst of it all thinking: I am a traveler now, just like all these others, and I am wandering no more.

I stride down Bagshu Road, find my little room for two hundred rupees a night in the Green Hotel. The room is closet sized, damp and mildewed, painted yellow with cracked concrete floor. Mismatched curtains are torn and faded and I can see right through them into the busy street below. There is a giant spider in my bathroom, as wide as my open hand, and she gets red-eyed and cross when I take a picture of her. I set aside old fears, name her "Clarice", call her my new roommate and just let her be.

The bed is a hard cotton futon mattress with a thin pillow and a dusty wool blanket at its foot. But as I look out the open door over the second floor balcony, down into the misty valley criss-crossed in prayer flags of white, yellow, red, green and blue I think this simple room is as good as a palace. I stomp my feet on the hard floor and clap my hands like some happy child. The Green Hotel is now my home.

All I want to do is lie down and sleep but I can't, not yet. It is almost noon and I am late. The teachings have already begun but if I hurry I will be able to get my admission pass and make the afternoon session.

Back down Bagshu Road I run, following the black lines of the map that is burned in my mind, all the way to the building marked Security Office. I am on the tips of my toes, humming a little victory tune as I walk through the door. I have made it! Ten thousand miles on this long, hard road. There is no stopping me now!

But then, without any warning, I *am* stopped, suddenly and surely and dead in my tracks. A giant chalkboard hangs at the far end of the hall and I narrow my eyes in the dark to read and re-read the tall letters that spell out in clear and perfect English:

THERE ARE NO MORE PASSES FOR HIS HOLINESS' TEACHINGS.

"There must be some mistake," I say out loud.

I close my eyes, imagine the website that I thought I had checked and double-checked. *Passes are only issued on the first day of the teachings,* it said.

There is obviously some translation problem at work here, so I scurry from door to door peering into the tiny rooms looking for answers. But no one is home. Then I hear a stirring towards the back. In the very last office sits the only stern Tibetan I have ever seen. He gets up from a rickety wooden chair and looks me up and down. I have lost the ability speak so I wave and sign in unintelligible gesticulations. I try to tell him that I want a pass for the teachings; that I have just gotten off the seventeen-hour bus ride from New Delhi and the fifteen-hour flight from America. I pantomime the past year of preparations and planning and hard work. I explain in sweeping, arcing gestures all the magic and synchronicity that has led me here, to this very place, at this very moment.

He is unmoved.

"Didn't you read the sign?" is all he says.

"Yes," I manage in a whisper.

He turns shaking his head and leaves me standing there alone in the dark hall. There is no earth under my feet. There is no sky above. I do not know where I am or why I have come. All I know is that I am crushed, I am devastated, I am without hope. I am stuck in India for two months and already something has gone terribly, terribly wrong.

McLeod Ganj wakes early outside my window, tossing off the blanket of monsoon mists as the sun begins to rise. It starts with a stirring just before dawn. A Tibetan voice whispering loudly in the alley. The feral dogs nipping and skirmishing for scraps. Truck drivers quarrelling over the right of way down the narrow street. They end their little disagreement by calling each other *bhai*, 'brother' in Hindi, and so I roll out of bed with a hopeful smile.

The sinking feeling of the day before is gone and as I wake and stretch, I resolve to make the best of whatever comes to be. I tell myself that I have come too far to give up, even in the face of great disappointment. If I don't get to see His Holiness today, then so be it.

I remember a talk I had with a friend only a few days before getting on my plane.

"What will you do if you get sick?" she asked.

"If I get sick," I said wise and smiling, "that will be my experience of India and I'll just have to be ok with that."

I have to laugh now at the memory and I decide to take the dare, to take my own advice. Whatever challenges and disappointments I have to face, I will face them. Whatever karma I have accumulated, good or bad, I will accept it.

I take two quick steps to the bathroom on the cold concrete floor. I look into the scuffed, cracked mirror, see Clarice looking over my shoulder, and marvel at this new me. I look him in the eye and tell him how proud I am of him. I tell him that everything will be ok, that he is in India and that is enough.

Downstairs in the kitchen I feast on a hearty breakfast of milk tea, honey pancake, fresh apples and sweet curd.

By eight a.m. the sun is shining hot and bright through the clouds and I step out into the street once again. Even if I can't see His Holiness, I will go to the teachings anyway. Just to be near the place will be enough.

Today there is a flowing stream of monks, nuns and laypeople alike all making their way down to Tsug Lakhang, the main temple and residence of the Dalai Lama. We rush down the hill together until we come to a stop at the temple entrance, a swirling, eddying pool of spiritual seekers. Then we trickle through the main gate and soon the flow of bodies is rushing again into the heart of the temple. The way is lined with beggars and lepers. Flies buzz around their listless faces. They have hopeless, glassy eyes and weak, bony arms. They reach out to us all with their withered, wrinkled hands saying *please, please, help us please!*

This is *samsara*, the endless cycle of suffering existence.

We move through this gauntlet of heartbreak and sorrow, up through the outer walls of the temple. But now the air is filled with mantras that fall down on us and all the other lost souls like cool rain, washing us clean. The mantras are deep and ancient and the gravely voices of the monks lift all our hearts up out of our misery and confusion, if even for just a moment.

I come to the security line and without thinking I lift up my arms. A security guard passes a metal detector across my chest and waves me on.

"Wait, wait," I say. "What about a pass?"

"Passes are only needed for the main teaching hall," he says smiling. "Go, go!"

Confusion gives way to understanding then delight and suddenly I am a ten year old boy being let into Disneyland ten minutes after closing. I sprint up the wide stairway and by the time I reach the top, I am laughing and spinning into the open courtyard. There are a thousand people or more gathered on blankets, on little patches of grass, under the shade of small trees. There are Tibetan families, western seekers, Indian tourists, monks and nuns from all over the world. Children play with bright balloons in the middle of the courtyard, heedless of their parents' calls for quiet.

The morning's teachings are already underway. I hear the Dalai Lama's voice reverberating and crackling through the old bullhorn speakers, just on the verge of breaking out into laughter and it makes us all smile.

I find a seat on the temple steps. A Tibetan family makes room for me. I feel welcome. I am not a stranger here at all. At the midmorning break, they share butter tea and dense flat bread with me like we have known each other for years.

The morning teaching comes to an end and a hush falls over the crowd. Even the children have stopped playing in the courtyard. We all turn at once towards a wide flight of stairs on the right and wait until His Holiness the Dalai Lama, the spiritual and temporal leader of Tibet, a simple monk, comes into view.

We bow our heads as low as we can until a thousand brows graze the earth at once. Then there is silence, deep, vast and pregnant with reverence and even the wind in the trees takes pause. He is one who has walked the path. He is, in fact, the path itself.

In the silence I hear that familiar laugh and I can't help but look up. He moves through the sea of bodies, bent with age but with uncontrollable exuberance. He breaks away from his attendants every few feet to offer a handshake and a melodious laugh to everyone within his reach. It seems that no one is a stranger to him.

As he climbs into the car that will take him across the courtyard, back to his residence, I look around at all these people and realize that none of us are strangers anymore. We are all here for the same reasons: to let go of our selfishness and to embrace love and compassion as a way to bring a little more happiness into this world. We are all pilgrims really, stumbling as best we can along the way while hopefully leaving behind a little more baggage with each mile we travel.

His Holiness is still smiling and offering his blessings to the crowd as the car pulls away. Our eyes meet for a split second. It is not the perfunctory eye contact of politicians and celebrities but a genuine reaching out. For that brief moment I know he is looking just at me, taking the time to really see me. He smiles, then I smile back. I melt and dissolve right there before his eyes until I am completely content and for the first time in my life I am certain that I have come the right way.

On the last day of the teachings the sun shines through a circle in the clouds that has hung over the temple for five days. Each morning the rains have threatened to pour down on us but every morning they were held at bay as if by some unseen power.

At morning tea monks step gingerly through the crowd, filling our cups from great pewter pots and tossing fresh bread into outstretched hands. It is the loaves and the fishes and the Sermon on the Mount rolled into one and we are living our own myth right here and now. I timidly reach out my hand but the loaves fly over my head. An old nun with brown lines that run across her face like happy valleys and rivulets reaches out, pokes my arm and smiles. She tears off a chunk of bread and hands it to me. I dunk it in the hot, salty butter tea and take big, chewy bites until my belly is full and warm.

When the teachings come to an end, there is no feeling of loss or sadness but instead a great uplifting and rejoicing. White offering scarves in the hundreds and thousands fly through the air, blocking out the sun with a canopy of silk. They float silently from the back, land on my shoulders and brush across my cheeks. I pick them up and help them on their way, throwing them forward into the rolling waves that lap at the base of the temple.

I laugh and smile at the beauty of it all, and for a moment we are all one family.

Now there is one last ceremony. His Holiness calls on us to kneel and so with everyone else I do; I who balked for years at kneeling to anyone or anything. But now it is time, time to let go, time to take refuge. My heart races as it finally dawns on me that this is the whole reason I have come here.

Up until now I have not called myself a Buddhist. I have hedged around the question, even while knowing the answer beyond a doubt in my heart. It is so much to live up to, such a great claim. I do not want to let myself down.

For twenty years I took refuge in drugs, in sex, in fleeting moments of relief. I took refuge in my loneliness, in my hopelessness and my despair. I took refuge in the lies I told myself and in the fiction of myself that I had written down in painstaking detail.

But now, that fractured self, healed and whole, is finally able to declare something with irrefutable certainty. And so I repeat the words that the Dalai Lama asks us all to recite: *I take refuge in the Buddha. I take refuge in the Dharma. I take refuge in the Sangha.*

And like that, it is done. Nothing has changed. Everything has changed.

I walk back up the hill. I am a Buddhist now. There is a clap of thunder right above me. Huge drops of rain fall from the sky, slapping and stinging my face. Soon the street is a rushing river of flotsam that washes the whole earth clean. Monks in red robes unfurl rainbow umbrellas and dart up the hill laughing. I blink my eyes once, then twice but they are still there and all I can do is stand with open arms as the rain comes pouring down.

Chapter 20

The Pilgrim

*There will be hardships enough to make my hair white, but I shall
see with my own eyes places about which I have only heard. I
shall be fortunate if I but return alive, I thought, staking my
future on that uncertain hope.*
~ Basho

Varanasi. Banaras. The City of Shiva. The City of Light. The
holiest city in all of India.

I sit on the rooftop of my hotel overlooking the Ganges as the
sun, rising higher and higher, sears my skin through a lens of
haze and pollution. I look up river, to the north, squint my eyes
and wipe away the sweat. No one is coming for me. Not yet,
anyway. High above the banks of the river I am safe.

Only minutes ago I was running, running like I have never
run in my life. I must have looked terrified. A *sadhu*, a holy man
sitting close to the great river, looked at me as I sped by, his eyes
wide, reflecting the fear in mine. Then he laughed, thought I was
just scared of the burning *ghat* a hundred yards behind me;
another westerner, sheltered from the sight of death, running
now like he's just seen a ghost. But that's not it at all.

Yes, I saw the place. Mani Karnika Ghat. Great piles of
burning and death, stacks of wood three stories high, the faces of
the buildings charred black and turned brittle from centuries of
consuming fire. *Feed the fire, feed the fire, feed the fire, say the gods.*
The sight of it burned into my mind. I stood there transfixed
while the rise and fall of my chest slowed until no breath came
and went at all, just like the bodies wrapped in white cloth there
on the pyres.

"So these are the fortunate dead," I thought.

To die here in this place is the great wish of all Hindus. This place so close to heaven that illumination is granted to anyone who does. The old and the sick, if they can, make their last pilgrimage here. They wait to die high up in the dark rooms of the hospice. They wait for their bodies to be transformed into smoke and ash at the river's edge, before they are offered back to the Ganges, the source of all life.

It is terrible. It is beautiful.

I knew well how sacred this place was, knew that to even be standing here as an outsider was barely tolerable. I knew too, that to take a photo of this place was the worst kind of brazen insult. But as I looked out and saw the other tourists flashing away, safe on their hired river boats, I just couldn't help myself. So I took out my camera and holding it low like a spy, snapped a single shot.

"Give me your camera!" came the shrieking voice.

I looked up and saw the wild-eyed young man coming towards me. He must have bounded down through the piles of ash while I had looked away to put the camera back in my pocket. He was wiry, scrawny and before I knew it he was right in front of me hissing through jagged teeth, cracked and stained brown. His clothes were covered in soot and ash. He was one of the *chandalas*, one of the untouchables, one of those that burn the dead.

"Give me your camera," he hissed again. And so I did, too scared to refuse.

He turned it on and scrolled through the images. When he saw the one I had taken he huffed in disgust and shoved it back into my hands.

"This is a holy place," he said. "You do not take pictures here. That is the hospice; people are waiting to die there."

"I know, I know. I'm sorry, I'm sorry," I said, face red with shame. "Look, I'm deleting the picture..."

"That's not good enough!" he screamed. His voice rose,

spinning and spiraling into a storm of rage. "Now you have to make a donation to the hospice...thirty thousand rupees...no! Sixty thousand dollars!" Foam and spit sprayed from his mouth. I couldn't move.

"You come with me now!" he demanded. "You come with me now or...or...I will get all the people up there to come down and... they will smash your camera!" His fist smacked his open palm in front of my face.

The future flashed in front of my mind's eye. I would soon be surrounded by the angry mob and they would not stop at smashing my camera. No, they would tear me into little pieces and toss them into the river where there would be no final illumination for me.

He turned and waved me to follow. I took one step in his direction but when my right toe touched the ground in front of me, I pressed it hard into the earth and pushed off into the opposite direction. And so I ran, sprinting along the walkway on the Ganges, running as if for my life in the morning sun.

Back at the hotel, I finish my breakfast, peering over the edge of the rooftop patio. There is no angry mob marching along the riverside hunting for the rude barbarian. I laugh. Then I scold myself gently. I remind myself that I am not here to gawk. I am not here to nose my way into lives private and sacred. I am not really even here to see this great and ancient city but rather the tiny suburb of Sarnath, the site of the Buddha's first teaching. It is here, a thousand miles from McLeod Ganj on bus, train, taxi and foot, that I will begin my pilgrimage to the four holiest sites in all of Buddhism.

Now I take the next step. I gather my supplies for the day: water, pen, paper, camera. I head into the labyrinth of alleyways and narrow streets that is Varanasi. It is an ancient mess of a city. It has been burned to the ground centuries ago and rebuilt, almost deliberately it seems, to confound any sense of direction.

I am swallowed up by the place immediately and as I tumble and twist down its gullet I pull out the hand drawn map that the hotel concierge gave me. It is nearly useless as alleys dead end and passageways disappear as I pass them by. Lofty stone houses rise up all around me like giant waves and they push me always just off course.

Somehow, I make it to the main road and the square. The alleyway opens up and I can see the sun shining bright in the blue sky. The city quakes and trembles and vibrates under my feet. An ocean of pilgrims crashes on its walls while a billion more voices and minds call out to it from afar. Yet still it stands, immovable through time, accepting this great crush of bodies and faith like some divine mother.

I look out onto the bewildering crossroads and it seems that all of India has gathered here. And in a way it has. Tomorrow is Diwali, the last day of a month long festival and celebration of the great hero Rama's victory over his evil brother Ravana. This is India's Christmas, New Year and Fourth of July all rolled into one. Fireworks have been going off all night. The whole city is shopping for gifts and sweets and the square throbs and bustles like Times Square in December. I am smashed and smooshed and pressed into the flow by the hundred thousand bodies that are all around me. I can feel the heat of their breath and the smell of sweat fills my nostrils until I swoon. I can't decide if I want to laugh or cry or dive back into the maze and run to my hotel in terror.

The rickshaw *wallahs* see me waver and in seconds I am surrounded.

"Where are you going? I will give you best price!" they all shout in chorus.

"Sarnath," I say.

I am pulled and pushed and grabbed. I am merchandise. I am gifts for Diwali. I am food on the table.

One young man pulls, pushes and grabs more fiercely than

the rest. He fights the others off with better English and more resolve and they are forced to move on to easier prey.

"Sarnath," he says smiling. "My rickshaw is the best. I will take you there for five hundred rupees."

Haggling. It is an art that I do not understand at all. Ever since I got off the plane from America five weeks ago, the bewildering web of unfixed prices and etiquette has been a constant source of anxiety and uncertainty. I have no idea what anything is worth. Sometimes a banana costs more than a train ticket or a hotel room. The dance begins with the merchant quoting an outrageous price, five or ten times what the item or service is worth. Then it is the buyer who must be resolute and shrewd, dueling with the merchant until an equitable price is reached. I have yet to make sense of any of this.

But now I feel a swell of confidence. The hotel concierge told me to pay no more than one hundred and fifty rupees, about three dollars, for each way of the ten-mile journey. Finally, with the certainty of something's value, I am firm.

"That's too much," I wrinkle my nose and do my best to appear insulted. "I'll give you three-hundred at the most."

He slashes at me with a steely glare. I have shown my hand too early. I am an amateur and now he knows it. With a fatherly *tsk-tsk* this twenty year-old boy cuts me to pieces.

"No," he says with finality. "That is too little. I must spend the whole day taking you there then waiting to bring you back. I will lose a whole day's work because of you. Five hundred, no less."

I nod my head. Of course. How could I have been so selfish? My will crumbles under the spell of his reasoning and I happily agree to the ten-dollar price. He is, after all, doing me a favor.

The rickshaw flies through Varanasi like a buzzing cicada. The streets are choked with a mind-boggling gridlock but the driver, Sunil, has no fear. He swerves in and out of the traffic without letting off on the gas. Even if the brakes do work on this rickety machine, he doesn't use them. He leans on the horn, plays it like a maestro. He composes a concerto of staccato rhythms and ascending glissandos that seems to conduct all who hear it to the side of the road.

We speed through the great din and confusion and I am laughing in the back seat with the wind in my face. Sunil looks in the rearview mirror and laughs with me. Everywhere on the road there are sacred bulls and cows. A hundred thousand pink and gold and glittered gods fill the stalls of the street vendors. Shiva and Shakti, Ganesha, Vishnu and Kali all dance through the streets to the Hindi pop songs that blare from every speaker. This is India and I am in love!

Soon the streets become wider, lined with giant shade trees and lush, green gardens open up on either side. The traffic thins to a trickle and soon we hum along alone. The calm of the suburb of Sarnath is a sudden shock but as I take in a deep breath of the fresh air, I am glad.

We come to the taxi stand just outside Mrigadaya, the Deer Park. I pay Sunil half the fare up front. I will meet him back here in three hours, and he will be well rested and well fed.

I set off on foot into the park, through the gate and onto the tree-lined path. Then I see it, there through the branches of the trees. My heart races. I can hardly believe I am here as I run down the path. I can't wait to get up close to the thing, to touch it, to feel the hard stone with my fingers and feel the weight of its presence before me.

The Dhameka Stupa. Built by the great Mauryan emperor Ashoka in the second century B.C. The giant monument marks the exact spot of the Buddha's first sermon, the First Turning of the Wheel of Dharma. It was here that the Buddha came after attaining Enlightenment in Bodhgaya, two hundred miles to the east. The legend goes that he came to the Deer Park searching for the five ascetics, his companions from his days of meditating in the forest. At first they pointed at him and jeered:

"There's that slacker, Siddhartha. He couldn't handle the life of an ascetic. Look at him. He's well fed and wearing a clean robe. He's not on the spiritual path anymore."

But as he came closer the five companions knew that something was different about their old friend.

"Gautama, you look changed. What's happened to you?"

"I am no longer the one called Gautama Siddhartha," he said. "I am awake." And from then on he was called the Buddha, the one who woke up.

I am out in the open now, the Great Stupa only yards away. I take each step slowly, deliberately and I cannot take my eyes off the thing. It is massive, with a gravity of its own and it pulls me in. One hundred and twenty feet high and more than that around. Silent, ancient stone and brick adorned with exquisite carvings of birds, flowers and human forms. My mind is stretched back farther than it ever has been, two thousand and five hundred years.

I am right before it now and as I reach out to touch it, cool and rough in its own shade. I half expect the thing to shock me with its power and energy. But there is nothing. Once again, there are no revelations, no mystical awakenings. There is just the peace and the quiet of the Deer Park as I circle its base.

And so I walk and so I pray. Still self-conscious, still uncertain. But the beads of my mala slip across my fingers a little more easily now and the prayers I have memorized flow swift and sure under my breath.

May my spiritual practice flourish for the benefit of all beings.

May I never again be separated from spiritual teachers in this or future lives.

May my generosity, loving-kindness and compassion develop to their full potential so I may be of the greatest possible benefit to others.

I round the thing once, twice, a dozen times. Is this all? Is this enough?

Through a hole in the fence that borders the park three young boys slip in. The oldest and most brazen of them runs right up to me. He pushes a booklet of postcards into my chest even as I pray.

"These are the best postcards," he says, a little out of breath. "Only fifty rupees."

I flip through them casually, not wanting to buy anything, trying not to feel annoyed. But there in the middle there is a full color photo of Mani Karnika Ghat, dark and forbidding with fires smoldering in the foreground. I laugh through my nose.

"I'll give you twenty," I say and the deal is done.

The Deer Park is nearly empty now as I amble around. Outside the tall fences that surround its border, scores of women reach their arms through the black iron bars. They are skin and bones wrapped in colorful silk. Many of them have skinny babies hugged close to their breasts and they sign to me that they are hungry. My eyes meet the gaze of an old woman. Her eyes are glassy and yellow and from twenty feet away I can see they are bloodshot and tired. I try to look away but I can't.

"Hello...sir..." she croaks. "Sir...hello...hello...hello..." Her hand reaches out to me, hanging there limply in a gesture of pleading, resignation and hopelessness.

I am confounded. I am in shock. I have no idea what to do. So I just keep walking while the woman calls out to me louder and louder as I get further and further away.

The Buddhist texts say that the pilgrim should come to the holy sites with an attitude of reverence and awe. I have cultivated that in plenty, but now, as I leave this first stop on my pilgrimage, I am more confused than illuminated.

With a furrowed brow, I leave the Deer Park. I find the taxi stand and Sunil is waiting for me. He is cheerful. He is glad to see me. I am a good haul for him. On the ride back to Varanasi he lets it slip that he only pays two hundred rupees a month to share an apartment with three other students from the university. I feel used, betrayed. I am a fool and a sucker. When he drops me off in front of the mouth of the old part of the city I give him the rest of the fare plus another two hundred rupees, four American dollars. Baksheesh, it's called; gratitude for services rendered. I am trying to let go, to show myself that the money doesn't matter. But there is an undercurrent of disdain. His eyes light up as he levitates out of his seat. He will have a good Diwali.

I pull out my little map, crumpled and damp with sweat, tearing at its edges and folds. I turn it, rotate it, flip it upside down. The map is simple. A few main roads all heading east. No reference to the web of side streets and alleyways that lies before me. My eyes follow the tiny arrows marking the path that should take me directly to my hotel. Straight in and to the right. Simple.

I look up and see thousands of people rushing on foot in and out of the main artery of the city. They are dressed in their finest holiday clothes, flowing silk and glittering gold. Sometimes they bunch up at the entrance before starting to flow again. I wait for the tide to rush back then I jump in and am swept away. Within fifty paces I am completely disoriented. I think I should still move to the right but the city has swallowed me up again. There is no up, down, right or left. There is only the noise and the smells and the lights and the throng.

I hesitate outside the entrance to a small spice shop, looking down again at my map when thick fingers grab me around my arm. I look up into a jowly, smiling face topped off with a mop of greasy hair. Winding rivers of sweat roll down its neck to a bare chest.

"Yes! Come. Sit! You want spices? We have the best spices. My brother here will get you some!"

He plops me down in the middle of the tiny shop on a roughly carved wooden stool. The shop is a broom closet, every inch of wall lined with shelves stacked high with glass jars filled with spices. My nostrils fill with the rich aromas of cinnamon, cardamom, chili and turmeric.

The skinny brother starts to happily fill up little plastic bags under the glow of a single bare light bulb dangling overhead. Soon the *garam masala* and *tandoori* are piling up before me.

"No, no!" I say. "Really, all I want is one..."

"Why so little?" Big Brother says with a sneer. "What? You don't have any money? You are from America right?"

"No...it's not that...I just..." My breath quickens and the blood rushes to my face. I look over and Skinny Brother is not listening to me at all. He happily drops bag after bag of spices in front of me.

"Look!" I shout. "I don't want all of these! I don't want *any* of these!" I pull my shoulders back, puff up my chest and move to get up out of my chair. I want to scream, kick, bite, punch and throttle. I fight them in my mind.

"Oh, you have very strong body," Big Brother says, puffing up his chest in mockery.

Skinny brother points to the mala around my wrist and laughs.

"Ah, you Buddhist," he says as if that says it all.

The brothers laugh and joke in Hindi. They point at me and shake their heads. "Buddhist" they say again and again.

Compassion? Patience? Generosity? Loving-kindness? These become flimsy concepts that blow away in this tiny breeze of anger. They are nice things to think about but here in the cramped space of a spice shop in Varanasi, I see I have few of these qualities. The words ring hollow now. I was a fool for coming here.

I throw down a handful of crumpled rupees, pick up a bag of spice and run back out into the maze. The brothers' laughter rings in my ears. People are everywhere, coming at me from every direction. Their faces are strange, their clothes are strange, their voices are strange.

Again I try to force a path to the right but always I seem to be driven to the left. Still I dive in, in to the heart of Varanasi. Now the shops are becoming fewer and further apart. There are no more western faces and I start to take in deep, quick breaths as the walls of the city close in around me. Soon I can't even see the sky, just ancient wet stone that I can reach out and touch on either side. The alleys become narrow passageways and I have to mash my body flat against the walls to let young men on motorcycles and cows squeeze by.

I stop to take a sip of water. I am tired. I am hungry. I am lost in Varanasi.

But then I start to laugh. How can I be lost? I have found my way to the banks of the Ganges from a small city in Colorado. I take a deep breath now and let it slowly fill my lungs. My heart slows too. I feel my feet pressing hard against the firm earth. It is the same earth that I have stood on back home. The warm sun shines on the back of my neck over the rooftops behind me and I close my eyes and hum to myself.

I jump off of the ground a full six inches. The Sun! It's setting! I am facing east! If I keep heading this way I have to reach the river! The revelation sends me skipping and whistling through the labyrinth. I move quickly now and surely with the sun always to my back, pushing myself off the walls with my fingertips as I zig and zag.

Soon, the faces become friendly again. The eyes of little children light up when they see me coming, the lost westerner.

"Hello!" they shout with glee, the only English they know.

"Namaste!" I cry with open arms.

I see now. For just a moment I see. There is nothing to fear. There are no enemies here, only the ones in my own mind.

I turn a corner. A cool breeze kisses my face. There, at the end of the alley is a great black cow. She looks at me, carelessly chewing cud and swatting flies away with her tail on the edge of a sheer wall. Then she looks back over her shoulder, over the wide river that glitters with countless drops of sunlight. I walk right up next to her, look over the edge and see that it is not a wall after all but a long, steep flight of steps. I fly down them in great leaping bounds, laughing out loud all the way to the river's edge, laughing like a child at the sheer delight of it all.

Chapter 21

Bodhgaya

One day a musician met the Buddha and asked him for instruction on how to meditate.

"Is the sound of a guitar best when the strings are very tight?" the Buddha asked.

"No," the musician answered.

"Is the sound best when the strings are very loose?" the Buddha asked again.

"No," said the musician.

"How is the best sound produced from the guitar?"

"When the strings are not too tight and not too loose, but just right."

"Then you should meditate like that," the Buddha said finally. "Not too tight, not too loose but just right."

The Mahabodhi Temple is before me now, a massive spire reaching up into the clear sky from a deep well of eternity. If there was a call that had been ringing in my dreams for the past year, this is the place of its origin. But I am wide awake now. The stone is hard, smooth and real under my bare feet as I take each slow step down to the place. An endless stream of pilgrims flows around the base of the temple and I dive into the current, letting it carry me along.

"All the earth is sacred," a fellow traveler told me just this morning. "All ground is hallowed ground." He was trying to convince me that we don't have to come to Bodhgaya to be in a holy place.

"That may be true," I had thought. "But if so, why are we here?"

I come around to the south end and when I see the Tree for the first time I am stunned into silence and awe. I have to step out of the current as bodies rush into me from behind. I stagger backwards, a waving hand reaching out behind me, groping for support. My heels bump against hard granite and I fall down onto a low seat sitting there, out of time, until it seems that even my heartbeat stops. Utterly silent and composed, I am filled with the certainty that each step I have taken for this past year has been on good, solid earth and has led me to a good, solid place.

This descendent of the Bodhi Tree stretches her long, dangling limbs over me, just like her forbearer did over the Buddha two and a half thousand years ago. Her leaves shimmer and twist and dance in the warm breeze. Sometimes a score or more of them break loose from her branches and spiral down to the earth. Pilgrims swarm, giddily snatching them up before I can even think about rising. A young Tibetan monk, ten years old, picks one up that has landed right in front of my feet. He has an armful of them already and he cradles them to his chest like precious jewels. He is about to return to the stream but when he sees me looking on longingly, he turns and with a happy smile and bright eyes drops every last one of them into my lap.

Generosity. Compassion. Loving-kindness. Letting go. All of the teachings of Buddhism that I have been picking like ripe fruit for these past months now explode in my mind. Suddenly I clearly understand why I have come here. To practice, to prostrate, to pray!

A sense of profound urgency swells inside me. I have wasted too much time already. Twenty years flailing and thrashing in the wild ocean of addiction and fear. But no more! I put the precious leaves one by one into my journal to keep them safe. Then I return to the stream of pilgrims, back into the current, back into the flow of devotion and faith.

I circle the temple round and round, ticking off thousands of *Om Mani Padme Hums* on my mala. I offer expensive flowers, incense and robes to the golden statue of Shakyamuni Buddha inside. I meditate on love, compassion and emptiness on the hard, cold floor until the sharp stones cut into my ankles. I send out desperate wishes for all beings to be happy until my head aches and throbs. I want to do a million practices of devotion, today, right now, to prove my sincerity once and for all and I check them off, one by one, like a laundry list.

But still, it is not enough.

With the sun high in the sky, I wander through the garden outside the temple, through the stupas and banyan trees. A spiraling galaxy of thick wooden planks, each one the length of a human body, radiates out from the Tree. In another month, when the cool of winter settles over the plains of Bihar, all of these will be claimed as thousands of devotees bow thousands of times to the axis mundi of Buddhism.

But now they are empty and the grove is still, hot and quiet. I look over my shoulder. I am not alone. There, in the corner of the garden, is a young woman. Her blonde dreadlocks fly through the air as she throws herself down onto one of the planks again and again. She looks right through me as she brings her hands to her forehead, throat and heart before descending in one fluid motion until she is outstretched on the prostration board beneath her. Then her hands come sliding back to her sides and she pushes herself back up. She repeats the bows in a steady rhythm, eyes open and never wavering from the Tree.

I find a board of my own under the shade of small banyan tree. I wipe off the dried leaves and dirt, stand solemnly and erect at the foot of it. Then I begin. My hands slide into the grooves on the hard wood, worn deep and smooth by a hundred pilgrims before me.

When I push myself back up for the first time, the chanting begins as if on cue. A group of Tibetan monks sits in front of the Tree. They have been silent for a long while but now their prayers resonate through the grove like the deep hum of the universe.

The melody and rhythm spur me on and I think: *this is it, this is the sign!*

I want to do a thousand prostrations, a hundred thousand. I want to become enlightened right now. Soon I am pouring sweat under the zenith of the sun. The air is thick and humid. I am pushing myself too hard. I am afraid that this time will slip away but the harder I grasp on to the experience the faster it does. My face is flush and I feel like I'm going to fall over. I sit down and sip slowly on my water. Then I close my eyes and try to catch my breath.

It is early afternoon, bright and hot as I leave the temple. I have been here since early morning, prostrating, chanting, offering, meditating. I am winding the string of my practice too tight, not wanting to waste a second, wanting to do this "right".

My stomach rumbles and growls but before lunch I want to mail a handful of post cards back home. I discretely pull out a small map of Bodhgaya. I know that if I am seen looking even the least bit lost, I will be surrounded by a dozen young Indian men and boys all clamoring to be my guide.

The map is clear: keep walking down the market road, then to the left. The post office should be right around the corner. A short stroll through a strange land. I look at the map one last time for courage then fold it away.

"Hello," the young boy says. He has silently rolled up next to me on a rusty old bike with fat, squishy tires. "My name is Sonu. What are you looking for?"

"The post office," I say. The hairs on my neck bristle and the blood rushes to my face. I don't want a guide today and I brace myself for the inevitable parry that is to come: *Let me be your guide,* he will say. *Only two hundred rupees...*

"I can take you there," he says before I can protest. I look him up and down, then over at the six other would be guides who have begun to gather around us. Sonu is smiling up at me. My senses, on overdrive in this foreign place, tell me the boy is genuine and that I have nothing to fear.

"Ok," I say. "Which way?"

He leaps and laughs then he grabs me by the arm with one hand, his bike with the other. He leads me through the market, bustling with the intensity and chaos that is always India. The air is filled with smoke and the buzz of mopeds that zip in and out of the narrow, crowded streets. The cows and bulls nudge me out of the way when I pass them too close. A thousand merchants sell their wares from tiny plywood shacks or on dirty blankets laid out on the ground. Fresh fruit and trinkets; cell phones, Coca-Cola, plastic gods and incense. Rivers of silk, all saffron and sky and gold, pour out of the tailors' shops while their ancient sewing machines whine and whir under their pedaling feet. There are teashops and sweets vendors, swindlers and conmen. My head spins and all I can do is laugh in my delight.

The minutes stretch out like taffy but still we walk on. I think we should be there by now and I look again, unsurely, over at my young friend. There are no western faces but mine anymore and the whole town is staring at me now as we pass. I am consumed by the delicious fear and uncertainty and excitement that have become a new and healthier addiction for me.

"Here it is," Sonu says triumphantly.

I walk into the old rotting building. It smells of mildew, dust and disrepair. The paint peels off the walls behind the high teller counter and the ceiling fans wobble and rattle overhead. A despondent clerk looking like a worn out cog in the great wheel of Indian bureaucracy, waves me over from behind his tarnished brass cage. I show him the postcards and shrug.

"USA?" I say in my tourist's broken English.

"Sixty-four rupees," he drones.

I hand him a hundred-rupee note but he frowns.

"You don't have change?" he asks. No one has change in India, not even at the post office.

He hands me a pile of stamps. I fix them onto the cards and hand them back. In two weeks they will make it over land, air and sea back home and it will seem like a small miracle.

I can't help but smile broadly at this little success. Everything is new, fresh and exciting on the road. Even the simple act of sending something off in the mail becomes some great victory, a red-letter day, a milestone that will never be forgotten.

Sonu is waiting for me outside, leaning against his bicycle and whistling softly to himself.

"Easy, no?" he says.

"Yes, easy," I say.

We walk together back towards the temple. We pass again through the mess of shops and merchants.

"Chris, will you buy me a soccer ball?" he asks suddenly.

Here it is. The con unfolds. The indestructible and all-important "I" crystallizes into a solid mass of indignation and resentment. I want to kick and scream and run away. But then I look over at Sonu. He has no shoes. His clothes are dingy and frayed. It is the middle of the day in the middle of the week and he is out guiding an unfathomably wealthy tourist, a bartender from America, to the post office.

"Sure," I say. "Where can we get one?"

He is ecstatic when I hand him the brand new ball. Two hundred and fifty rupees. Five American dollars. A rip-off but I do not feel cheated. I hold Sonu's bike while he bounces the ball off his feet, head and chest and laughs.

"Chris, do you want to see my school?" he asks as he tucks the ball under his arm.

I am tired and hungry. All I want to do is eat then find a cool place to lie down out of the midday sun. But I am here. When will I ever come back to this place? I remember that I vowed at the beginning of this trip to say yes every step of the way, to stay open, to not shut anything out. I look down the road and can see the temple behind the trees. I could make it back to the main road easily on my own. But instead I follow the boy as he beckons me with a wave and a smile.

We leave the market and dive down a little dirt path that leads us into a sprawling shantytown. The single story homes are nothing more than plywood shacks with scrap metal roofs and dirt floors. Curious faces peer out of dark doorways and windows on either side. Gangs of teenage boys spill out of side streets and alleyways to gawk at the pale American.

Every twenty yards we pass the shrines of Hindu gods and goddesses. The statues inside them are seven feet tall, all surrounded by offerings of fresh fruit, flowers and burning incense. Earsplitting Hindi prayer music screeches out of antique bullhorn speakers, praising the kindness and glory of the gods.

We turn a corner and I come face to face with a towering image of Kali, the goddess of Destruction. She is grisly and fearsome. Thick black hair sprouts wildly from her head. In one of her four hands she holds up high a great curved sword, in another a man's freshly cut head. Around her neck and waist are garlands of severed heads and limbs. Her mouth and tongue drip with blood as she dances gleefully on the corpse of her consort beneath her feet. She is beyond life and death, beyond mind, a doorway to the transcendent but in the bewildering maze of the shantytown I do not see this. All I see is terror and ferocity in her white, piercing eyes.

Now all the faces we pass become filled with menace and malice. Sweat pours down my neck, my back, my chest. I am being led into a trap. Soon we will turn down a dead end where a gang of wild, desperate men will carve me up with rusty knives and machetes. My body, an offering to Kali, will never be found.

"Chris," Sonu says reading my mind. "Don't worry. Be happy."

He reaches out and takes hold of my hand. I look down and see there is no malice in his eyes and the fear melts away. Then I look into the faces of the people we pass and see they have been smiling the whole time.

We come to a courtyard and the children from the neighborhood instantly surround me. Sonu shows me off like a prize. The children poke and prod me until they are certain that this strange looking man with sunburned skin and red hair is real.

"Come, Chris," Sonu says. "Come see our school."

He leads me into one of the shacks, into a small room. I have to bend down low to get in through the doorway. It is a tidy little one-room schoolhouse. The dirt floor is swept clean. Tiny plastic chairs are stacked in one corner. Sonu pulls one down and offers me a seat like an honored guest. There is a desk that a teacher might sit at, a large map of the world hanging on the wall above it. On a shelf beneath a square hole in one wall that serves as a window are books, paper, an old tin can filled with pens and pencils.

The children scurry to different corners of the room, pull out prized objects and show them to me.

They are just little things, maybe left behind by travelers like me, souvenirs that have become learning aids, artifacts that prove that there is a world outside of the shantytown. A postcard, a piece of quartz, a magnet, a coin from Australia. They come to me one by one and in perfect English give me lessons in history, geography, geology, economics.

"This is from Czech Republic," Sonu's friend says proudly showing me a postcard.

"Do you know where that is?" He points to the map on the wall and I think the boy has a clearer image in his mind of that place than most people I know back home. There, they still call it Czechoslovakia.

Their energy swirls around me and I feel dizzy. They seem to know more about the world than I do. I look into their faces, see that they are hungry to learn. But there are no classes today. No lesson plan. No teacher.

Sonu hands me a fat scrapbook filled with letters of authenticity from others who have sat in this seat before me. They testify to the children's tenacity and dedication. They implore me to stay here, to change my plans, to offer whatever help I can to these eager students. So I rearrange my life in my mind, extend my trip for another six months. I see myself sitting behind that desk until the summer comes around again. But then, on the last page is a registry with names and donation amounts. The fantasy dissolves like sugar in water, sweet to taste but not good to drink.

And so I take the easy way out. I pull out a crisp five hundred-rupee note and try to hand it to Sonu.

"No, no," he says like I've just tried to give him a loaded pistol. "Never give money to children! They will gamble with it or play cards."

He leads me out of the schoolroom and to his house across the courtyard. His mother is there cooking over a small, hot fire of burning buffalo dung. She follows us as Sonu leads me into the dark shack. There is not much for my eyes to adjust to. Home is a single room. There is a bed where his mother and father sleep, another for he and his nine other brothers and sisters. I look around in disbelief. With three of us in the room it already feels cramped and close.

I give the money to his mother. She stuffs into a little box on a high shelf.

"Chris, can you give us a thousand rupees to buy rice?" Sonu says quickly, eyes darting away from mine.

Suddenly, Sonu is no longer Sonu. Now he is the ten-year old pickpocket I saw the other day at the temple. He is one of the fake *sadhus* pressing me for more alms than I want to give. He is all the young boys in the market who latch on to the rich westerner hoping for a hand out. He is the masses of lepers, the poor, the sick, the hopeless. He has a million arms, a billion arms and they all reach out to me crying, "More, more, more. Give us more!"

"No, Sonu," I say sharply. "Just because I am from America doesn't mean I'm rich." And as soon as I tell the lie it's me that has to look away and hang my head in shame.

"I'm sorry, Chris," he says and doesn't bring it up again.

Sonu takes me by the hand one last time. We are friends again. I am exhausted and hungry as he leads me back to the road in the late afternoon. I glance over at him from time to time. He is whistling his little tune and I marvel at how he can be so happy. I blush as I think of all the limitations I have forced upon myself in the past, of everything I've squandered. I realize now that I know little of limitations and difficulties. I look down at Sonu and see that he doesn't have much choice in his life at all. Wish as he might to get an education, or to become a doctor, or to one day leave Bodhgaya, he will never do any of those things.

He brings me to the cul-de-sac at the entrance to the Mahabodhi Temple. Monks and nuns and pilgrims encircle us as we say our goodbyes. Finally, I let go of Sonu's hand and begin to walk away. I turn to wave one last time but he has already disappeared. I have missed the point entirely. Yes, it is good to meditate, to prostrate, to pray. But what good is this if it doesn't help those in need?

So I follow the road that leads back to my comfortable life feeling a little bit guilty and even ashamed. But then I remind myself that the road is hard. It's not meant to be easy. What's easy is to miss what's important, to get lost in the land of the Self. So I speak gently to myself again. I let go of the guilt. I decide that all I can do is use what wealth I have without letting it control me. I will give what I can. I will try to use my gifts wisely.

Chapter 22

Kushinigar

Life is short and the time of death is uncertain, so apply yourselves to meditation.

~ Milarepa

I am on my way to Kushinigar, the place of the Buddha's death, and at three in the morning I pace up and down the trash-strewn platform of the train station outside of Bodhgaya. It is nearly deserted and I feel more alone and out of place here in the dark and the cold than I have in all my time in India. From the open sewer of the tracks below comes the stench of urine and rotting. Giant rats scurry from track to track while great flapping wings of mysterious reptilian birds whoosh through the black sky. Monkeys screech and scream at one another from the trees in the dark.

But for the kindness of strangers and my few words of Hindi, I am not overwhelmed by a rising panic. Little English is spoken or even written here. The departure board said that the Budh Purnima Express will leave in forty minutes from Platform Four. But when I show my ticket to the sleepy-eyed railway worker he shoots me a puzzled look and points to Platform One with a shrug.

I strain my ears towards the garbled departure announcements that blare intermittently over the crackling speakers:

"Your kind attention please," comes the nasal voice. And then a mess of muddled Hindi and English consonants and vowels spills out into the chill morning air.

"Excuse me," I say to a lone passenger. He is a young Indian man strolling up and down the platform with his hands in his pockets.

"Am I on the right platform?" I show him my ticket. He takes it in his hands and looks at it, wrinkling his nose. He spins it around, upside down, flips it over then hands it back to me with a long, slow *hmmm*.

"*Tin*," he says in smiling Hindi. Three.

I run, frantically, up and over the walkway to Platform Three, my backpack slicing into my shoulders as it bounces up and down. It is three thirty five. I am going to miss my train. I will be stuck in Bodhgaya forever.

A headlight shines around the corner in the dark. The train rolls to a slow stop and a few bleary-eyed passengers pour out. There is no announcement, no number on the train. I get on and find what I think is my seat but when the conductor looks at my ticket he shakes his head.

"Budh Purnima Express," he says. "Very late." He pushes me out, back into the dark and onto the platform.

The few passengers that have gotten off the train have already spirited away into the night and I am alone again in the dark and the quiet. I let my backpack slide off of my shoulders and I sit cross-legged on the cold platform next to a pile of filthy rags.

But it is not rags at all. Suddenly, it begins to stir and unfold. I leap up, ready to run down the tracks in fear as a human form uncurls itself from underneath a torn t-shirt smeared with dirt and grime. It is a young man, no more that twenty, already broken beyond repair. He is all bones now, sharp at the joints that threaten to tear through the wrinkled brown paper sack that used to be his skin. His wispy beard and wild, black hair are a nest for lice and leaves and bits of trash that have come to rest there.

He struggles to move and each bending of each brittle limb is a creaking agony. I think he might be dying right then and there before my eyes. I glance feverishly up and down the station, looking for someone who will rush to his aid. Someone must come.

But there is no one. There is only me.

I stand frozen as he pushes himself into a squat. He holds his knees, wobbling over the ground as his bladder lets go. A stream of urine splashes into thick muddy pools around his feet. His face twists and contorts in burning pain but his eyes show no sign of emotion: they just stare blankly into the space in front of him. It is as if the human being that once occupied this body left it long ago to fend for itself.

I am no more than ten feet away. I could take two decisive steps and help him to his feet, take him to God-Knows-Who, to someone, to anyone for help. But I don't. All the meditations on compassion, the wish to free others from their suffering and pain, are sucked out of me like air into the vacuum of space. Instead, I stare, jaw dropped open, like a dumb, mute statue of stone. It takes long, slow minutes for him to rise to his feet and when he does I think the cool breeze coming from the north will blow his hollow bones and paper skin down the tracks.

As the apparition staggers off and disappears around the corner, I wrap the memory of him neatly into an unlabeled box and hide it away on a lonely back shelf in my mind. By the time my train comes four hours later, chugging and steaming around the tracks, I will have already forgotten him.

I thought that pilgrimage would propel me forward, that there would no longer be any hesitation or doubt. But on my way out of Bodhgaya, I am afraid to go on. The reality of India is in my face screaming at me all the time that the world is big and complicated and full of pain. There are few happy endings or simple solutions. It's almost become too much for me to handle and I think, not for the first time, of taking the easy way out. I could get a flight to Kathmandu, skip the overland journey to Kushinigar and Lumbini and just leave India behind. Two out of the four pilgrimage sites will be enough, I think. The Buddha will understand.

Seventeen hours later the train is pulling into Gorakphur, the last stop before Nepal. I have come too far to turn back. The inner voice that has propelled me on through the past year and a half whispers to me softly yet firmly: *Keep going, do not quit, you can do this, I love you.*

It is ten thirty at night but the town is still sweating and shaking in the endless fever of India's activity. Cows, rickshaws, taxis and bicycles all barrel down on me as I leap across the road.

I fly up the stairs of the Elora Hotel and the night clerk is just about to turn off his light when I stumble, breathless up to the desk. He shows me to the last vacant room and when he turns on the light I feel the walls crush in around me. A narrow, dirty hall leads to the cramped bedroom. The walls are crumbling plaster, damp and mildewed. A red, flashing light strobes through a single window, smoky and opaque from fifty years of pollution. The air is still and stifling and I immediately begin to pour rivers of sweat.

"I'll take it," I say.

At this hour I know there is little possibility of finding anything better. I unload my pack and look into the bathroom. There is the familiar sight of the squat toilet. The smell of raw sewage fills my nostrils as I begin to wash up. When I turn on the faucet a flood of cold, brown water splashes around my feet from the dangling pipe underneath the sink. But I am unfazed. I have been on the road in India for six weeks now and I am a seasoned traveler. I dig the little roll of duct tape out of my pack that I have carried along with me for ten thousand miles. I climb under the sink and reattach the pipe. Victorious, I let the water run clear then splash it on my face and even defiantly brush my teeth with it.

It is late now and all I want to do is go to sleep but when I come out of the bathroom and take a closer look at my bed, my heart sinks. The low-lying mattress is jammed into a dark corner of the room. There on the walls are dozens of reddish brown smears of blood. I lean in close, see that they are the crushed corpses of bedbugs that have gorged themselves on previous guests only to pay with their lives.

I look down at the cold, dirty tile floor then back at the bed. I dig through my pack again, find the bottle of powerful insect repellant, slather the toxic goo all over my body until it burns and stings. I imagine it seeping in through my pores, into my blood stream, mutating my cells. Despite the heat, I put on a long-sleeved shirt and pants and lay my chemically treated sleeping bag on the bed. I turn off the light and lay down, careful not to disturb the sheets that are tightly tucked around the mattress.

So there I lay, clutching my flashlight close to my chest, turning it on like a spotlight at the slightest sound. And with the ceiling fan *clackety-clack-clacking* above me like a crashing helicopter, I finally fall into a fitful sleep.

I wake, stiff and rigid, in the same position as when I laid down. I am off the bed and standing in one fluid motion. I check my face, neck, chest, legs. There are no bleeding bite marks or open sores. I have made it through the night unscathed.

My plan was to take a day trip to Kushinigar then return for one more night here in Gorakphur before making my way to the border. But all I want now is to get out of India. I have given it my all for a month and a half, tried hard to stay open, to not judge what I don't understand. But the intensity has taken its toll. I remember what a fellow traveler told me early on:

"The first time you come to India it just explodes inside your head."

It has certainly done that to me. Now, all I want to do is get to Nepal as quickly as I can, to find a quiet place to rest, to sift through the rubble and hopefully put the pieces back together again.

"How much to hire a private car to take me to Kushinigar then Sunauli?" I ask the clerk. The words come spilling out. It is six in the morning but he is already wide awake and open for business.

"One-thousand-eight-hundred," he says without pause.

Thirty-six American dollars. I was prepared to pay three times that much so I forgo even the pretense of haggling and tell him to make the call.

Elated by resolve, I float down the stairs to the street, buy a breakfast of bananas, biscuits and ice cold bottled water. Everyone is smiling in the early morning haze, everyone is my friend in India. Then I breathe in great draughts of humid air, perfumed with that familiar scent of musk, diesel and dung.

A young man, eyeing me from across the patio, braves the divide of culture and language and asks to take a picture with me. He smiles wide, mouth dripping with the red juice of a kind of chewing tobacco called *pan*. He puts his arm around me while his friend snaps photo after photo on his cell phone camera.

This is me and my friend from America, he will later say proudly.

My car comes for me, a maroon Tata sedan with skinny little tires and a pockmarked complexion of dings and dents. I climb into the back seat after taking one last look around, at the dirt and the pollution and the crowding and the chaos. Now that I have decided to leave it all I think I will miss it. But it is time to go.

I am laughing quietly to myself, so happy to be on my way, when the driver turns around.

"Did my uncle tell you about the highway tax?" He is smiling too, but it is not a friendly one.

The hairs on my neck stand on end. Blood rushes to my face. I know exactly what is going on here but I am cornered in the backseat. I want to leap at him now and pummel him with angry fists. I want to take out all my frustration on this, the darker side of India, the darker side of humanity. He is all the scam artists and con men and hard sells that have pressed all around me since I first got off that plane.

The driver turns forward and points us out into the endless flow of traffic.

There is a pounding on the roof of the car and the driver slams on his brakes. There, outside his window, is the clerk from the hotel waving his finger at him with a stern, knowing glare.

"No cheating!" his uncle shouts.

Now it is the driver's turn to blush and sweat. He mutters under his breath as we make our way out of the maze of streets. He cranks up earsplitting Hindi music, droning sitars and shrill, little girl voices, and looks away every time our eyes meet in the rearview mirror.

At the "toll booth" a group of desperate, wild eyed men standing by the side of the road get up to block our way. One of the tax collectors waves a fist full of bills in the driver's face while he stammers and stutters why I won't be paying the three hundred rupees today. Then the tax collector screams and shouts while he slaps his hands on the roof as gravel spits back at him from spinning tires.

For two hours we fly down the unpaved, potholed highway in silence. We shoot out of a cloud of our own dust that settles gently down on the broad palm leaves that line the side of the road. Once, they were green but now they are all covered in a fine sheen of chalky, powdered earth. Soon we are the only car on the dusty highway.

"*Apka nam kya hai*?" I say in Hindi breaking the silence. "What's your name?"

"Ajay," he says unimpressed, turning his eyes back to the road.

Finally we pull off onto a shoulder of grass next to the quiet town of Kushinigar, one dirt road lined with a restaurant and a few ramshackle shops.

"Which way is the Nirvana Stupa?" I ask.

Ajay waves his arm vaguely across the road and tells me we will leave in an hour. Then he walks away to find a place for his lunch.

An hour! I had hoped for at least two. I start to scurry, frantically around the town. There are no street signs, no maps with helpful "You Are Here" arrows pointing the right way. All the shops are closed and the town feels deserted. If I hadn't seen a sign for Kushinigar a few miles back I would think that I was in the wrong place all together.

I rush down little alleyways until I come to each of their dead ends. Then I run back out to the main road and trace my way around to the other side of the long row of shops.

There, gleaming in the sun is a great golden dome with a delicate spire that reaches up into the sky. It looks Thai or Burmese. I find the entrance and wander around inside the giant stupa looking for some sign of the Buddha's passing, a marker, a statue, a stone. But there is nothing here, just a dark, cold circle of a hall hung with canvass paintings depicting the Buddha's life.

Back out in the sun I look desperately around for other pilgrims. But the place is empty. I look down at my watch. Thirty minutes have already slipped away and I start to panic. I run towards town again but something tells me I am going the wrong way. So I turn hard on my heel and run back to the Burmese temple, back to the line of trees that I saw behind it.

Through squinting eyes I see a narrow path in between the giant oaks. I run for it and through it and finally out into a wide and rolling field.

And there it is, on a raised foundation of brick and mortar in the middle of the field, amidst the ruins of ancient monasteries. The Nirvana Stupa, the place where the Buddha finally passed away into the Great Expanse. I can almost see the peaceful ghosts of the monks that used to watch over this place, still sitting there in their long contemplations of the passing of all things.

Hindu pilgrims, in pure white and crimson, spill out into the yellow afternoon from the little shrine that sits in front of the stupa. I walk up the brick steps and into the shrine myself, against the outflow of bodies. There in the middle of the little hall is the reclining Buddha, twenty feet long, covered in gold leaf and red silk. He is surrounded by pilgrims, eyes closed, chanting soft prayers under their breath as they walk clockwise around what they believe to be a manifestation of Krishna. Some throw offerings of silk onto his body that float down like cascading flower petals.

I am mashed up against the walls and I do not enter the flow. I reach up with my camera, take a few snapshots then leave the place with a vague feeling of disappointment. I had wanted the Buddha all to myself, to sit there quietly with him and just be.

As I step out again into the early afternoon haze, exhaling long and slow, I smile. I am getting used to this lack of epiphany, this lack of revelation. But now it is enough to breathe in deep the peace of this place. A gentle breeze brushes my face and the troubles of the outside world are swept away. The pilgrims are all smiling at me and me at them as I walk around to the stupa.

It is a simple white concrete dome, just an unassuming bump on the face of the earth. If I didn't know what it was I might just walk right past it; another monument to this god or that, lost in time. But I *do* know what the meaning of this thing is and as I round the circular base, saying again the mantras, I am slowly filled with enormous gratitude. I am here! I am alive! I have survived!

My thoughts drift back to just this morning. We had passed a typical Indian town: crowded, noisy, dirty, almost unimaginably remote and poor. The streets were lined with tiny shops made of bamboo and brick, all of them black from soot and diesel. What if I had been born here, I thought. What would my life have been like?

There would have been no working hard, diligently saving my money to make some grand pilgrimage to America. There would have been no coming out to family and friends. There would have been no tolerance for being gay at all. There would have been little chance to discover Buddhism even in its homeland. In fact, there would have been little chance to do anything but follow the clearly prescribed life of tradition and caste. Maybe I would have wound up on the side of the road extorting money from tourists or I could have been the Starving Man withering away from hunger and indifference on a cold railway platform in the dark.

But instead I was born in the West, in America. I am free in ways that I am only beginning to understand and appreciate. The life I lived before, suffering, afraid, alone and in the closet is now behind me. My life now is nothing less than blessed. I can do whatever I want. I can walk for miles on my two good legs. I can breathe and smell the clean air. I can feel the sting of my disappointments and longings. I can take a step back from them so they don't sting as bad. I can think and discern. I can read and write. I can study, travel, learn and live whatever and wherever I wish. This truly is, as the teachings of Buddhism say, a perfect human rebirth.

My watch beeps softly but still loud enough to jar me out of my meditation.

"So this is pilgrimage," I think as I rush back down the steps and to the path.

At the line of trees I stop and turn one last time to look back over the holy spot. It rests there in the quiet, a reminder that all things change and die, even the Buddhas. My time here is so short and so precious, I think. Then I turn and run.

Chapter 23

Lumbini

One should first earnestly meditate on the equality of oneself and others in this way: "All equally experience suffering and happiness, and I must protect them as I do myself".
~ Santideva

Here, at the end, I have come to the beginning. Nepal. Lumbini. The place of the Buddha's birth.

It is a fine, warm morning in Bhairawa as I leave my hotel in search of the bus that will take me to the place. I step out onto the sidewalk and stomp my feet on clean concrete, do a little hopscotch skip down its length. Sidewalks! A simple thing I had forgotten to miss these past weeks. The faces I pass on the street now are round and soft with bright eyes and smiles. Gone are the austere, intense faces that I have grown used to. Here, in one of the poorest countries in the world, the people seem at ease. I take in a deep breath of the peace, let it fill my lungs and exhale, for now, the memories of India.

"Lumbini?" the young man asks as I approach the bus stop. There is only one place a westerner like me could be going so he waves me onto the decrepit old coach. Its tires are worn to the threads and it creaks and groans as I step up to find my seat but when the driver cranks up the engine, it turns over with a fierce growl and soon we are bounding along dirt roads far out into the country.

No matter how full we get, we take on new passengers at every stop. When there is no more room inside they climb onto the roof. We sit close and cramped, knees and arms pressed together, unafraid of one another, human family one and all. We let out great peals of laughter as we hit huge potholes and all of us lift off our seats, suspended in free fall, our guts jostling and doing somersaults in our bellies.

My forehead knocks out a little drum roll on the window as the villages of Nepal pass by; little gardens of paradise. A father kicks a ball to his young son. People shop for groceries at sidewalk markets. They eat in restaurants, call friends on cell phones, check their email in rustic Internet cafes. They wait impatiently for the bus, fix flat tires by the side of the road and assure their children that they will be ok when they fall down scraping tender knees.

I am a million miles from home. I am not far from home at all.

"Lumbini, this stop," shouts the driver over the engine's roar and all the tourists and pilgrims climb out.

The path is lined with trees. They look like eucalyptus with smooth, pink bark and oval serrated leaves that spiral down in the breeze. There are a few pilgrims already gathered at the start of the path. We are Indian, Nepalese, European, American, Buddhist, Hindu and Jewish. We are young, old, gay, straight. We are healthy. We are dying. We are solemn. We are joyful too and we all walk towards the temple now, giving each other space in the late morning.

It is a long path but I take each step slowly. Sometimes I look down at my feet, listen to the *thwock* of my flip-flops on the gravel and the dust. Sometimes I look up at the clear blue sky. I am not here to rush, or too push too hard, or to wind my strings too tight. Not here; not today.

A great slab of white marble inscribed with English letters rises up in front of me. I stop and read.

I observe refraining from killing any living being.

I observe refraining from taking that which the owner does not give.

I observe refraining from committing sexual misconduct.

I observe refraining from telling lies.

I observe refraining from taking any intoxicant or drug.

I think that these, the precepts of Buddhism, have been

written just for me. It seems so anyway. A million memories of mistakes, misjudgments and miscues of a man and a life gone astray flood through me. All the lying, stealing and cheating. All the mad, desperate fucking in rhythm and sorrow. All the suicides and the hundred thousand days and nights lost in the fog of a lonely sedation.

My belly tightens and twists into the familiar half hitch of regret but here, I resist the impulse to pull it tight. I remind myself that I have made my amends and I will continue to do so. My life from this day forward will be my amends. So for now, I will follow these precepts as best I can, like vows, saying them softly to myself every morning before I throw off the sheets and step into the new day.

Now here I am at the end of this stage of my journey. Mahadevi Temple. The temple of the great mother. A square house of red brick built over the ruins of a more ancient memorial that once stood here. Inside it is dark. It smells like moldy earth. As my eyes adjust to the light I see catwalks meandering over partially excavated ruins. They lead slowly to the green stone that marks the spot where the Buddha was born. Above it, there is a statue of Queen Maya giving birth to her son, miraculously, out of her side. The figures of mother and child are worn and smooth and they gaze eternally down at the spot across the chasm of twenty-five centuries.

Is this really the place? I look down at the stone and wonder, does it even matter? I don't think so. Alone in the dim light of the temple, I close my eyes. All the pilgrims who have come here through the centuries, through greater hardship than mine, stand around me in noble company. In the still and the quiet I can hear them whispering a billion prayers and sincere aspirations. A chill runs through me as I realize that I am one of them now.

I bow my head low in respect then turn towards the door. It is done. I have come all this way only to realize that it was not a place I was looking for but the purification of my soul and of my intention.

Outside, a great Bodhi tree stands watch in front of a man-made pond, illuminated under the zenith of the sun. Brightly colored prayer flags stream down from its branches and trunk, fluttering happily in a cool breeze. I make my way towards it slowly, steadily.

A bearded mendicant in white and orange robes sits under the canopy of green. He smiles at me out of his meditation as I pass. Next to him, a shrine of candles, flowers and incense rests in a natural altar between the strong roots of the tree. Someone knew this: the earth is a holy place and so are the trees and the stones and the still waters.

A pile of straw mats is neatly stacked on the other side of the tree and I unroll one and take a seat on the ground. This is the center of the earth and I plant myself firmly on it with my head reaching high into the sky.

And so I meditate with the old yogi, like a child imitating his wise old grandfather. First, I settle into my body, feel the breath rise and fall. I relax and breathe and let go. But meditation is not just sitting, blank and still in some vacuum of the mind. It is activity and awareness and contemplation. I listen to my heart and remember a meditation we did on retreat. The meditation on equanimity.

"Yes, that's the one," I think.

I recall the instructions, visualize in front of me three human beings: a friend, an enemy and a stranger.

The friend is before me now and a smile comes to my lips as all the memories of our connection unfold. The laughter, the favors done, the shared experiences, the respect we show each other. We benefit each other, we make each other happy. So we call each other "friend".

But as I look deeper I see that this label is neither fixed nor permanent. I think about all the friends I have had in the past. So many of them are enemies now. Some I have hurt so badly that they will never speak to me again. I imagine doing the same to this friend. There is every possibility that I could start drinking and using again, that I could become selfish and cruel again, that I could steal from her, betray her, throw away her friendship for a drink or a hit. Nothing is certain or guaranteed.

I move on to the stranger, a shapeless, nameless face that I can barely make out in my mind's eye. It is the passerby on the street, the clerk at the grocery store, the beggar on the side of the road. It is all the people I pass by everyday without ever giving them a second thought. Weren't all the friends I've ever had all strangers at one time? What changed? A tiny kindness. A funny joke. A bold introduction. The deeper I look, the more certain I am that every person I could ever meet has the potential to become a friend.

Now my enemy appears before me with all his glaring faults, all the qualities that infuriate me, all the reasons I think he deserves to be miserable. He drinks and lies and cheats and steals. He berates my friends with all his bitterness and bile. But here, in the quiet of meditation, I try to see him in a different light. I imagine how I would feel about him if he did me some great kindness. What if he saved my life or the life of someone I loved? Stranger things have happened in this world. I imagine how grateful I would be, how, if even for a moment, my hatred for him would melt away. I imagine forgiving him for all his perceived shortcomings and how for that one instant he would be the most important person in the world for me.

Slowly, I begin to see the point. None of us are fixed in place. We are always changing. It is only me that labels people as friend, enemy and stranger, not because that is inherently and always who they are but because of my own petty and shortsighted prejudices. I see now that all of these people are really the same. They are all looking for the same things in life. My friend wants happiness for herself and her family. My enemy wants the pain of his life to stop so he drowns it out with drinking and rage. All the nameless strangers I have ever passed by want nothing more than to live their lives in peace. Each and every one of us, according to our best wisdom, is simply trying to avoid suffering and gather as much happiness as we can get.

I open my eyes. The air is warm now even under the shade of the great tree. The old yogi is still there next to me. I smile at him serenely and even a little bit dumbly. Here, at the end, I am at the beginning and for just a single moment, after so much hardship and enduring and ten thousand miles, I know what it means to stop striving, to let the world and everyone in it just be.

I am full of light. Not perfect or pure or holy. Just light and I cannot stop smiling as I get up and walk with gentle steps back down the path to the bus stop.

The bus pulls up at the end now. I hear the fierce old engine rev and growl. I sprint the last fifty yards, kicking up dust and tiny stones. They sting the bottoms of my feet but that doesn't slow me down or keep me from laughing out loud as I rush past the guards, their heads snapping up from afternoon catnaps.

"Bhairawa?" I pant a little out of breath to the young man standing just outside the bus.

"Yes, yes. Bhairawa," he says with a huge smile. "Get on!"

Chapter 24

Trail Wisdom

I am on my way to the Himalayan trailhead for a short vacation after my long pilgrimage, but now my practice of Buddhism is being put to the test. Letting things be is not always that easy.

Our little bus grinds its way up the winding, narrow road and we twist and turn our way higher into the mountains, sometimes coming within inches of cliff edges that drop off into deep, rocky ravines. I look over the edge and am forced into a favorite Buddhist contemplation: the reality of impermanence and death.

Like all Nepalese buses this one it is packed to overflowing but still, at each stop, we load on whoever is in need of a ride. Farmers and villagers press in through the narrow doorway climbing over me like I'm a sack of rice, stepping in my lap, on my head, on my shoulders before squeezing into whatever room is left in the back.

Pemba, the young man who will be my guide on this ten day trek in the mountains, sleeps peacefully next to me, his head bouncing up and down on my shoulder. He is oblivious to our brushes with mortality and to the noise and to the smell of wood smoke and sweat. He is oblivious too, I think, to my receding anger.

"Our bus, I think it's leaving." He had said it like an afterthought a few hours before, a casual observation so that I didn't even look up from my plate of spicy potatoes. But when he and our porter leapt up from the table and out into the brittle Kathmandu dawn I felt their swell of panic.

"What do you mean you *think* our bus is leaving?" I called after them.

But they were already gone, out into the chaos of the bus depot and the thunder of fifty diesel engines all turning over and revving up at once.

I watched helplessly as they ran into the melee of the early morning commute, desperately slapping their open palms on the side of each bus as they roared out of the station. Each one looked the same, all adorned with sequins and pictures of Hindu gods and goddesses. Even the names of towns and destinations, printed in colorful Devanagari letters across the top of each of them, seemed to be useless. It had taken us thirty minutes to find the right one in the first place. Then Pemba somehow convinced me to load my pack onto it and leave it there while we had our breakfast.

I stood there in the cloud of choking dust and fumes imagining everything I owned being carried deep into the heart of Nepal. At first I told myself that everything would be ok, it was only stuff. I still had my money belt after all... But then the anger boiled over inside me. Soon all I could think about were *my* clothes, *my* camera, *my* toothbrush, *my* journal. Suddenly, all these little things became irreplaceable and I clutched at them tightly in my mind. I was entitled to these things and it was all Pemba's fault for losing them. I wanted every thing back and if I didn't get it all back right then and there, someone was going to pay.

"Motherfucker!" I screamed. An old Nepalese man looked up, startled, from his paper then walked away. I stormed around the parking lot, like I was the only person in the world, heedless of the roaring fleet of busses all around me, swearing under my breath. I could not see or hear or smell or feel anything at all. All I could see was Pemba's face in my mind apologizing over and over. And over and over again I watched myself punch him right in the nose until the blood trickled hot and red over his lip.

Zelu, the porter, found me like this, wild and raging, kicking rocks into the street and muttering to myself. He offered me a nervous smile but kept a safe distance from the crazy American, red-faced and hyperventilating. I shot him a fake grin through gritted teeth then crossed my arms and turned away like a child throwing a tantrum.

Then Pemba came running out of the dust cloud. He was smiling and he held up his hand as he caught his breath.

"What are you smiling about?" I was about to say as I clenched my fists.

"Our bus," he said pointing to the back of the lot. "It's still over there. I made a mistake and thought ours was leaving. All these Nepalese buses look the same."

Then he laughed. Then Zelu, slapping my shoulder, laughed with him. I looked down at my clenched fists, let them slowly relax and open. Then with tears welling up in my eyes, I laughed too.

We are passing a shepherd and his flock of goats now. The bus crawls slowly through them but does not stop. Our driver stops for no one on this treacherous mountain road. Pemba stirs next to me, woken by the change of pace.

"Where are we?" he asks groggily.

I don't really know so I just shrug my shoulders as he looks around and out through the windows.

"Ah, we're not even in Dunche. There is still a long way to go." He folds his arms and nestles himself back into his seat and again falls asleep while I stare out the window and smile. A long way to go indeed.

We are at Lama Hotel at seven thousand feet and I am walking back from the outhouse, knees locked and extended like some transplanted Frankenstein in the cold Himalayan night. It is only the end of the first day on the trail but I am already a quivering and broken mess. My knees feel like someone is driving fat ten penny nails right in through the bone. I am sick too with diarrhea from a bad meal in Kathmandu. It came on in a surprise assault on the trail and I am seriously considering retreat. I am not sure if I will be able to go on in the morning.

As I crawl back up the steps to my room all I want to do is give in to despair as I remember what an older German trekker told me at dinner:

"The trail is hard going for the next two hours," he said, "but then it levels out nicely."

I don't think I will be able to go on for two minutes.

I heave myself up onto the hard mattress and curl into the fetal position but even that fills me with blinding pain. I rock myself back and forth as memories flood back of all the training I did back home, hiking hard in the Rockies with a loaded pack day after day. Now, even with a porter to carry my things, I was barely able to finish this first and easiest stage of our journey.

Pemba had told me this trail was considered moderate, that the really hard ones require ropes and oxygen. I had to laugh at this. Sometimes this "trail" is not even a trail at all. Jagged, slick slabs of rock climb up the face of the foothills like Stone Age steps and sometimes the trail just disintegrates into wide sloping fields of loose gravel and scree. All the while Pemba and Zelu, wearing cheap tennis shoes, march up and down in front of me like they're on a smooth-gliding escalator. I look down at the feet of the Sherpas that pass by us with hearty calls of "Namaste", lugging up huge loads strapped to their heads and see that they are wearing nothing but flip-flops if they are wearing any shoes at all.

It is cold and dark in my room. There is no electricity. There are no blankets on the hard, flat mattress and I can feel the cold, howling wind blowing through the cracks in the walls. I curl up in my lightweight sleeping bag, wincing every time I try to move my legs. It takes me hours, but finally I fall asleep.

In the morning, Pemba is cheerful in the dark, smoky kitchen of Lama Hotel. He orders me breakfast from the proprietor who works over the clay wood stove, artfully moving black cast iron pots back and forth over the two open flames as he makes tea and hearty flat bread for all the hotel's guests.

"How are your knees?" Pemba asks.

"A little better," I lie. "But I want to go on."

He looks me up and down. If I can't walk, it will be he and Zelu that have to carry me back down the mountain.

"Ok," he says. "But I have one formula: continue slowly."

So we begin again. The trail looms in front of me, straight up into the forest. I take one step and already begin to sweat. I grind my teeth and groan as I take the next. After a hundred yards I am already falling well behind and Pemba looks back nervously. He lets me pass him to take the lead and set the pace. It is slow going and each step is filled with great effort but I am completely present in the pain and the motion and somehow this keeps me going. Soon I am not worried about how I will feel in thirty minutes or how far we will have gotten. I am here right now and I will not turn back, not today.

"Slowly today, one-hundred percent tomorrow," I chant to myself softly. The spontaneous mantra keeps me going and soon, my steps are more fluid, the pain less intense. Two hours later and sixteen hundred feet higher I am still going. My knees still throb but I think I might just be able to go on.

The high mountains are coming into view through the trees now and they call me forward so that I forget about the pain. These are the great mountains of the Himalayas. These are the gods of the earth and they thrust their bodies into the heavens watching over the world from on high. We come around a bend and like that we are above the tree line. I am stunned into awe by their mass and dignity that rise up all around me. They are capped in perpetual white and cold but they do not complain. I take a deep breath of the crisp, clean air and it is better than a long sleep. So we go on.

We stop for tea at a small lodge. A young Tamang woman, a cousin of the Tibetans only a few miles to the North, greets us as we come up the hill. She is chopping wood while her young son sits a few yards away, pulling up grass and flowers out of the earth then throwing handfuls of them up into the wind. This is a different world. The people here are hearty and resilient. I imagine becoming one of them, make a plan, a mental note to return home, sell everything I own and come back here forever. I sigh, longing and dreamy-eyed in the cold, dry wind pouring down from the mountains.

She invites us into the warmth of her kitchen, throws another thick branch onto the fire. She gives us each a small cup of *dahi*, yak's milk yogurt. It is sour and I wrinkle my nose as I slurp it down. The woman points at me and laughs.

"What are you laughing at?" I ask. I think she is laughing at the face I am making.

"She says you wear a bandana like a woman," Pemba says.

I have to laugh at this and my fantasy of becoming an honorary Nepalese crumbles.

"If you only knew..." I think to myself.

Then my heart sinks a little. I have idealized this place, this exotic world that I thought would be filled with Buddhist prayers and devout practitioners who had all long ago escaped the traps of prejudice and phobia. It turns out that this is a land of rigid traditions just like anywhere else. Here, on the roof of the world, there is little room for a man to wear a bandana on his head, let alone to be openly gay. I imagine all the challenges I would face every day here, making the decision of how and when to come out. But then I see that it is not the place that scares me. The truth is even coming out at home, where we have made such great strides in our quest for freedom and equality, still fills me with fear.

I look at the young woman with a growing suspicion as we finish our tea. Out in the cold sun we prepare to leave and I stare down at the ground, a little dark and distracted.

"How did you like the dahi?" the woman asks in slow deliberate English. It is the first attempt at my language she has made since we arrived.

"It was good," I say.

"In Nepalese we say *metta cha*." She is smiling at me now and I see that she is no enemy. It is my fears that I have to face and overcome, not someone else's beliefs or misconceptions.

"*Metta cha*," I say, slowly and deliberately just like she did. It means simply, "it is good". And so as we turn back up the trail and leave her behind holding her young son's hand and waving, I think there may be hope for us yet.

We are on our way down from Kyanjin Gompa and thirteen thousand feet and I am Dharma-less. Tibet, the Land of Snows, is only a few miles to the north but for me, the teachings of the Buddha are a thousand light years away. My knees are blown out and burning. Every step is stabbing pain and misery. I am wishing I never came on this hike at all when a couple in their sixties comes up the trail. They look happy as they make their way carefully up the hairpin switchbacks carrying their own packs. No porters. No guides. Just a retired couple taking a leisurely walk through the Himalayas. I am a pile of dry brush and they are a match and in a flash I am engulfed in the flames of resentment.

"How much money have I spent on this trek?" I ask myself. A thousand dollars at least.

Suddenly, I feel cheated, lied to. My friend in Kathmandu talked me into hiring these two young men to take me up into the mountains. He said that I would be more comfortable, more relaxed. Now, as we pass dozens of Westerners who are enjoying the journey by themselves, I feel like a fool.

"Hey look," I want to say to the old couple. "I'm not some snobby *sahib* here. These aren't my servants or anything. I just took some bad advice in town and now I'm stuck with them..."

But *Namaste* is all they say as they pass on by without looking back.

I know I should let all this go. Who cares what other people think anyway? But I can't let it go. Instead, I tumble down the hill in an avalanche of anger and suspicion that gets bigger and wilder with each passing step.

Pemba has me in front again, setting the pace, making sure he and Zelu don't push me too hard. Despite his kindness and concern I feel nothing but resentment towards him. Everything he does is amplified into a screeching cacophony of annoyance. The sound of his steps, his spitting and blowing his nose all bring me to the edge of violence.

Now Pemba is playing music from his cell phone and I am at my wits end. The Nepalese dance music blares out of the tinny sounding speakers until I can't take it any more. I stop dead in my tracks and he and Zelu pile up behind me.

"Could you please turn that off," I say.

"I'm sorry," he says. "Is it bothering you?"

"It's...driving...me...fucking...crazy." His eyes glisten like I just socked him in the nose then he turns off the music and hides the phone in his pocket.

"Sorry," he says. "I won't turn it on again..."

I turn and start the descent leaving him to wallow, I hope, in embarrassment and shame. We walk now in silence and the nastiness and the bile bubble up inside me until I can't see anything but swirling red and my feet pounding the earth in front of me. The beauty of the place still rises all around us but I am blind to it all.

We come to a high bridge that bounces and sways in the wind. I take out my camera and point it over the edge, down at the raging whitewater far below. In my self-centeredness I have forgotten Pemba is still behind me. But he is still there and he gently whispers to me to be careful with my camera, to make sure I use the strap around my wrist. When I turn to tell him to mind his own business, I slip on a patch of gravel and he catches me by the arm to steady me.

"Small rocks can cause you to slip," he says gently. But I just yank my arm out of his grasp and walk away without saying thank you.

The day slips by. We arrive at the lodge in the late afternoon. Zelu carries my pack up the steep steps while I wait at the bottom, helpless from the searing pain that still shoots through my knees. Then he comes back down and holding my elbow like the kind son of an elderly father, helps me up the stairs. I throw myself down on my bed and sulk. I am about to drift off into sleep when there is knock on the door.

"Sir, what would you like for dinner?" Pemba asks. "Especially, I think you would like the Sherpa Stew."

"Fine," I bark. I listen as the creaking steps fade into the silence. Then I toss and turn on the bed exhausted but unable to sleep.

The shadows in the room are getting darker and colder as the sun goes down in the mountains. I get up and hobble stiffly around the room. I fumble through my things, toss aside my journal, my books but I do not want to read or write. I find my camera, absentmindedly turn it on and scroll through the record of the past two days.

There is Langtang Lirung and the peak fills the tiny screen, massive and forbidding even now in the cup of my hands. We had hiked up to a little ridge to sit beneath prayer flags in the thin mountain air for a short while. There, under its twenty-four thousand feet of rock and ice, I could feel the peace and calm of the high places and why so many have gone there to meditate and taste the nature of the vast mind.

Then there are the "Woodcutting Men", the old-timers who shared tea with me around the fire. I showed them photos from back home and they whistled through their teeth as I proudly pointed out in broken Nepalese my brother, my mother, my father, my brother's wife.

There is Yangjen, the matriarch of Kyanjin Gompa Guesthouse, still smiling at me with shining gold teeth. She is making me a huge pot of butter tea, reaching over the wood fire, the hot flames licking her leathery fingers without any sign of pain.

I breathe in the memory of the peace of the place. There was no rush to do anything. All the tasks at hand were done with pleasure and purpose. The days were filled with cooking, making tea, sweeping the floors, stacking wood, getting water and tending to the small herd of wooly yaks that grazed on the brown hills. I remember the brightness in everyone's eyes and that even though they lived a simple life they were anything but simple themselves.

I remember the promise I made to myself that last night by the fire, to keep my heart, mind and senses open for the rest of my stay. My journey was coming to an end too fast. There was no more time to drift off in daydreams, or to lose myself in petty complaints about my knees or the little comforts I so often missed. No, for the next two weeks I would be completely present, a kind and respectful visitor, a happy guest in a beautiful land.

But today all of that resolve had flown off like a bird from an untended cage and four hours given over to anger and self-cherishing are now gone forever. I will never pass down that trail in the Himalayas again. What sights, sounds and joys did I miss as I sealed myself off from the world? More than two feet plodding in the dust in front of me, I'm sure.

My face turns red and hot as I remember Pemba and Zelu and my friend in Kathmandu now, how I had scolded them and turned against them. But now I realize that they have been working tirelessly for my benefit all along. Without them I would be lost. They have carried my pack, too heavy with things I don't need. They have found me the best places to spend the cold nights. They have ordered my meals. They have shared their language and their culture. One day, Pemba even told me that if my knees got any worse, they would gladly carry me back down the mountain on their shoulders.

I shake my head now in the dark. I have so much work to do. But I do not throw up my hands in defeat or give up. Yes, I have shortcomings but I will not beat myself up for them anymore. Instead, I will accept them and move on. I will be kind to myself and work hard to be better next time.

This is the practice. Watching my actions, watching my words, watching my mind every day. It does not only occur at holy pilgrimage sites or on retreats or in the presence of great spiritual masters. It occurs everyday, with the people who are with me right now, in this time, in this place.

I wipe away the few tears that have already begun to dry on my cheeks and crawl slowly down the steps to the main house. Inside, Pemba and Zelu are sitting by the fire.

"Hey, Chris!" Pemba waves to me with a big smile. "Come, your dinner is ready."

He wipes off a seat on the rough little bench and hands me a bowl of stew and when I look down into the steam and the goodness of it, I already know it will be the best meal I have ever tasted.

Chapter 25

The Narrow Way

Where we had thought to travel outward, we will come to the center of our own existence. And where we had thought to be alone, we will be with all the world.

~ Joseph Campbell

Mantras and prayers fill the air around the great stupa at Boudnath in the heart of Kathmandu. A hundred million words on wings. They are the words and aspirations of the faithful who have come to this holy place, this pure land, to pray for the well-being and ultimate enlightenment of all. They resonate not only today but from and through all the long ages that this place has been known to be sacred, a thousand years at least, far back in the memory of humanity, a memory continuously refreshed and renewed by pilgrimage.

Buddha eyes watch lovingly from the high spire of the stupa that reaches up into heaven. Prayer flags flap everywhere in the wind. Monastics in red robes circle the wide courtyard again and again, fingers nimbly, deftly counting off the beads of their malas. Gilded monasteries, topped with golden dharma wheels, sparkle in the sun. I am home.

I dive into the eddying stream of devotion once more, this time certain of what to do. *Om Mani Padme Hum. Om Mani Padme Hum. Om Mani Padme Hum.* I chant and chant until I am soaring high above the place, singing the words as if with a chorus that fills the whole world. If we would all sing this prayer just once, in every language and every faith, the wish for universal love and compassion would be granted I am sure.

An old nun sits on the low wall at the base of the great monument. She waves me in close as I round the circumference for the third time, taking hold of my hand, bringing it and my mala to her wrinkled, brown forehead, chanting a blessing in Tibetan. Then she sends me back out into the stream with tears of joy pouring down my face for all to see.

But the delight of spiritual ecstasy is impermanent, just like all things, and soon my rounds begin to slow. I am my ordinary self again and as I step out of the stream to look back at all the pilgrims absorbed in their prayers and inner journeys I am content, for now, to just watch and be.

My pilgrimage is drawing to a close but there is one last stop to make, one last stage of this journey that I must complete. High up on a hill above Boudnath there is a great monastery and it is there that I hope to find some answers and final direction, some kind of summation or validation for all I have done so far. Have I done everything I could possibly do? Have I said all the right prayers, made all the right offerings and aspirations? Has this journey meant anything at all?

I pull out a crumpled scrap of paper with scrawled bus numbers and street names I can't pronounce. Now, in the late morning, the square is filled with a great press of tourists and pilgrims. I cannot tell left from right, north from south or if the sun is high or low in the sky.

"Where are you going?" the young woman asks. She has been watching me from the edge of the square as I spun round and round in growing confusion.

"I'm looking for the bus to Kopan," I say. I hold out the piece of paper but she doesn't even look at it.

"No bus," she laughs. "Take the narrow way next to the little monastery up there to the left. Keep going up and you will find it."

The narrow way. Yes, that must be it. The Buddha found the Middle Way, the way between the extremes. It is my way now too, though I must be more careful not to step off of it, to keep on the line that leads me always forward.

I find the little path, squeeze in through the high walls that tower above me, further and further into the heart of the city until the place is utterly strange and unfamiliar. Muddy streets and close packed concrete apartments, the heads and limbs of their residents dangling from open windows. Myriad shops filled with electric gadgets and godheads, goat's milk and rice. Roosters and chickens strutting and pecking. The smell of cooked meats and smoke. The rattling of gasoline generators. The new and the old, past and present woven into a dense brocade of sprawling emerging world suburbia.

When I come to a crossroads, unsure of which way to turn, I think I will lose my resolve to go forward but there, standing on the corner as if she is waiting for me, is a western nun with grey hair and glasses. She is smiling and I know right away that she is a friend.

"Is this the way to Kopan?" I ask.

"Take this right," she says with a British accent. "When the road splits, stay to the left and keep going up. You can't miss it really."

She steps back onto the road and disappears into the maze behind me.

Again I plunge forward, skipping now and laughing. The road is wider and I can see a little more of the sky as I come over a hill. But still there is no monastery on the horizon. When the road comes to its split it heads down, not up, so again I hesitate.

A young boy stands by the side of the road with his hands in his pockets. I can feel his eyes locked onto me as I waver. My teeth grind loudly together as my chest tightens and my heart closes. He is another would be guide, another street kid looking for a handout and I do not have time for long negotiations and short cuts that lead me to his home, his school and the final pitch for help. Today I cannot play the *sahib* with a heart of gold. So I pretend he is a phantom, a ghost and I shut my eyes and hope he floats away. But when I open them he is still standing there, as solid and as real as ever. He does not disappear or evaporate into the high, yellow sun.

"Where are you going?" he asks.

"To the monastery," I say vaguely still looking straight ahead.

"Yes, yes. This is the way," he points excitedly down the dirt road that falls off to the left as if he woke up this morning hoping that today, finally, someone would just ask.

"Thank you," I say. Then I rush off hoping to disappear into the maze before he gathers the courage to follow.

But he does follow, though tentatively at first, waiting for me to invite him on my little walk up the hill. He is just behind me now, quick little steps barely keeping pace with my long strides. We both look straight ahead shooting cautious, sidelong glances at one another when we think the other is not looking.

"You...friend?" he asks finally breaking the silence.

I pause for a long while then give in and sigh.

"Sure," I say. "We're friends."

He is floating now, just an inch or two above the ground, with just enough lightness to keep up with me with his short legs. I think he is about to burst from joy and for a moment, I can't help but feel happy that he is happy.

"My name, Prabin," he says in English that shames my few words of Nepalese.

"I'm Chris," I say.

"Chrees," he sounds out the unfamiliar name slowly until he is content that he has it right.

He looks up at me and smiles then back down at the road in front of us. All he wants is to be my friend for a short while. Tonight, he will tell his family and neighbors about the red haired Westerner who he led up to Kopan. He will tell them with pride how he spoke English with him for hours, how he showed the lost foreigner his way.

But I don't know this now. I am too busy looking out for the pitch, the hard sell, the inevitable fee for this innocent friendship.

And so instead of laughing and listening and seeing the new world Prabin offers to show me with my two good eyes, I spend the time building little walls that keep the young boy out. And in so doing, I miss out on a lot.

I miss his pure joy as he shows off all the English words he knows: *my dog, my airplane, my motorbike, my mother.* I miss his delight and excitement as he points out the road to his home and his school. I miss the point when we stop at the ancient shrine of Ganesha where, with the reverence of a tiny high priest, he shows me how to fold my hands and bring them to my forehead in respect. I am too distracted by distrust to be awestruck by the smooth, worn statue of the elephant god, the wise son of Shiva, who watches over the little cave that leads deep into the heart of the earth and the home of the gods. As I clutch my money belt, I don't feel the sacredness of the earth under my feet, don't remember that every step I am taking is on hallowed ground.

"See? God," he says. Then he points to a neighboring stupa covered in Buddhas.

"See? Buddha god." But I miss the clarity of the lesson, the history of my new faith that is as old as the memory of all men and all women.

"This way Chrees," he says now leading me out of the shrine and onto a wide and rocky path. It is a short cut that leads back into the crush of the stacked cinder block homes of Kathmandu then out again across the main road.

I look up and there above us is the monastery, a sacred castle on a high hill. The short cut was not the detour that I expected and feared and now he leads me onto the narrow path that winds up the hill. It is steep too, and sometimes my face comes close to the ground in front of me as we climb.

At the top, sweating and out of breath, we come to a tall gate of steel and aluminum where a stern guard blocks our way. He looks Prabin up and down and shakes his head. His suspicion justifies my own but still I convince him that he is my guide.

Then he lets the façade drop and steps aside with a hearty laugh.

"Come in, come in," he says.

Prabin takes my hand and guides me through the monastery grounds like it is his own backyard. He shows me where the four hundred monks eat and sleep and pray. He points out every stupa and statue, giving little lessons and histories on each one. He leads me up stone steps to a high knoll on top of this already high hill. The whole Kathmandu Valley circles around us. I squint in the bright sun, point delightedly at Boudnath in the distance, see the winding road that has brought us here.

Prabin does back flips and cartwheels on the green lawn and laughs when I show him the photos I take of him. Then he sits down next to me on a little bench where we share water and the peace of solitude. Without a word, he reaches into his pocket, pulls out a plastic pen, puts it carefully into my hand and closes my fingers around it. I look down and shrug, then try to hand it back to him.

"No," he says. "Gift!"

I should be melting now and all the walls should come crashing down. All my doubts and suspicions should turn into mist and rise up and disperse into the wind. But I still don't get it and I put the pen in my pocket without another thought.

The tour is over now and we walk silently down the steps and back to the gate.

"Come," he says. "I take you back to Boudnath."

"No. I have to stay." I sit down on a stone wall, adamant and unmovable. I am here on important business. I want to talk to someone about matters of the spirit, about the way and the path.

Prabin looks at me longingly, asks me to come with him one more time. But he gives in to my resolve and finally steps back from the little waves of anger that are building inside me.

"Ok, I go now," he says.

He walks away, turning back to wave and smile every few steps. It is not until he turns the corner and disappears that I realize how foolish I have been. He is just a friend. No hidden agendas, no ulterior motives. He was just a young boy who saw a curious diversion passing through his day and decided to follow it for a while.

The monastery office will open at one o'clock. I will walk into the hot stuffy room, nervous and uncertain, and ask to speak to someone who can give me advice on my spiritual path. It will be a vague question, still unformed and stiff and the receptionist will squint his eyes at me, a little confused. But then he will flip through a list of extensions and call the right person for me to talk to.

I will follow his directions to the bungalow where the old nun will be waiting for me. She will offer me a seat on the couch outside her office and will listen patiently as I tell her my story. It will pour out in a hyphenated flood of words but she will still smile knowingly as she filters out the meaning. I will tell her the short history of the new me, freshly out and sober. I will tell her about the call of Buddhism heard loud and clear out of the chaos of the end of my old life. I will tell her about retreat and pilgrimage and everything I have learned so far. All the while she will smile and listen.

Then I will tell her about my plans for the future. I will return to America. I will study. I will practice meditation. I will work hard to prepare myself to return for longer retreats and serious devotion.

"Sounds like a pretty good plan," she will say with a sparkle in her eye. "What do you need advice on?"

Then I will breathe. A long, slow exhale and I will begin to let go. It is done. I have made it. The future is a possibility that I can only steer towards.

We will laugh for a while, share stories of pilgrimage and the lessons of India. She will tell me how far she has to go still on the path so that I feel humble and hopeful all at once.

"When one starts to wish for help on the spiritual path," she will say in the end. "Good things begin to happen. Things become clearer and the way opens up." Then she will give me a warm, encouraging smile and send me on my way.

The sun will be high in the sky as I step back into the open air and as I set foot on the walkway that will lead me back to the gate I will suddenly remember Prabin. He will have made his way back down the hill by now, back down into the heart of Kathmandu. He will be making his way home and as he gets further and further away my heart will lift light and free. Then, as it rises high into the clarity of clean air and sky, I will finally see that the path, just as it has always been and always will be, is right there in front of me.

MANTRA
BOOKS